A CELEBRATION OF

Flora and Fauna
of the Bible

A CELEBRATION OF

Flora and Fauna
of the Bible

ENDYMION BEER

with supporting text by Trevor Beer MBE

HALSGROVE
In Association with Naturama

First published in Great Britain in 2007

British Library Cataloguing-in-Publication Data
A CIP record for this title is available from the British Library

ISBN 978 1 84114 672 0

HALSGROVE
Halsgrove House, Ryelands Industrial Estate,
Bagley Road, Wellington, Somerset TA21 9PZ
Tel: 01823 653777   Fax: 01823 216796
email: sales@halsgrove.com
website: www.halsgrove.com

Printed and bound by D'Auria Industrie Grafiche, Italy

Contents

Foreword by David Bellamy   6

Preface   7

Introduction   9

Part One – Introducing the Birds of the Bible   11

Part Two – An Introduction to the Other Animals of the Bible   41

Part Three – Introducing the Plants of the Bible   93

Index   143

Foreword

A Fascinating potted flora and fauna of the bible. I always put them that way not because I am a botanist, but because without plants there would be nothing to feed the animals and that includes you and me.

The first interesting point to note is that temperate Britain shares many of the species with the warmer, drier climes of the Holy Land. What is more, the chosen lists of plants and animals would be equally apposite if writing a natural history of both the Queran and Talmud, the holy books of Islam and Judea.

Add to that the fact that many of both the plants and animals were, and still are important in the diets of the Eurasian stock that came north out of Africa to colonise Europe. Part of the diaspora of the descendants of Eve who wandered the world in search of other gardens of Eden.

Perhaps the most important was *Triticum Durum*, the wheat from which pasta is made, for this one plant helped settled agriculture to develop around well-watered spots such as Jericho. Onions and garlic are still prized to this day as cleansers of the human body and mulberry and pomegrenate good sources of antioxidants.

Then there are olives and grapes, mainstays of the healthful Mediterranean diet, although the nearest thing we come to the now ubiquitous tomato and potato both imports from the New World, was another member of the same plant family, the solenaceae.

Mandragorga Officinarum. The much feared mandrake now of Harry Potter fame. This poisonous plant was widely used in biblical times as a general anaesthetic during surgery and in the hands of a good herbal doctor all could be well. The effect of the anaesthesia was so strong that when out of kindess, the ladies of the Grand Sanhedrin administered mandrake to those suffering crucifiction the bodies of some, thought to be dead when delivered to their friends, were revived.

Herbals were the forerunners of texts on natural history listing the virtues of minerals, plants and animals first on papyri, fashioned from the white pith of the true bulrush of Moses fame, called byblos by Greek philosophers from which the word bible came.

Here is a delightful book to dip into and glean fascinating facts about the plants and animals that succoured those who found faith, hope and charity in the world's three great monotheistic religions.

David Bellamy
Bedburn, July 2007

Preface

As a naturalist-writer my brief from Endymion has been to give mention of the best known plants and animals of the Bible, and thus of the Bible Lands and to point to those either of the same species, or similar, in Britain and Europe. Thus, for example, the Badger of the Bible may not be 'our' badger but it may lead a similar lifestyle. Explaining this creates an interest in wildlife we may never see and brings the Bible itself closer to us. From the stories of the Creation, Noah's Ark, Solomon and so on, we can explore the Bible via its wild flora and fauna and perhaps feel the urge to know more.

This is not a textbook, it is written and illustrated as a guide, an entertaining journey through the Bible for the young and not so young that has the reader's love and enjoyment of natural history to the fore. Biblical Biodiversity, an all encompassing term for life everywhere, what the Creation was and is all about. It is meant to be a celebration of life, as is the Bible surely. Writing the text has certainly inspired me to find out more.

Note: Though this is not a scientific text book, but a celebration for all to enjoy I have included Scientific names of species where I felt them appropriate and useful to the reader. However, in view of the difficulties and varying opinions as to interpretation and identification of certain species, some 'old' scientific names may have been superseded by new ones over the years.

By Trevor Beer MBE
North Devon 2007

Dedicated to the meek
that shall inherit the Earth and to Mother Earth

Introduction

"…Help to make the world a better place and life a worthier thing."
His Majesty King George VI

Over the years many writers have produced beautiful books on the 'Plants of the Bible', 'Animals of the Bible', 'Trees of the Bible' and others. Some of these books are very old, beautifully illustrated, often with wood cuts, and gilt edged. Alfred. E. Knight and Rev J.G. Wood are two of my favourite authors and such books must be treasured for always.

Now, in modern society we are leaving behind our roots, forgetting the old ways and sometimes losing ourselves in the hurried pace that seems to be the way of today. How nice it would be to travel back to calmer more peaceful times. Since there are no time machines, perhaps a celebration of the Bible would be acceptable instead. So back to our roots….

I am not a scientist and do not intend to produce a scientific work. Instead, I choose to celebrate the Bible by selecting some of the flora and fauna mentioned and illustrating those species in colour. It isn't always easy to distinguish precise species since Linneaus was not around in Biblical times to give us scientific nomenclature. For example, it is believed the lapwing, as mentioned in the Bible, is actually the hoopoe. In this instance I have illustrated both species to explain this and have therefore illustrated other species as accurately as modern day translation permits, to produce a celebratory work.

I hope this book will be useful to the whole family. Those that are too young to read can look at the pictures (not to scale) whereas older children may like to look up the biblical references, thus learning about the Bible and how it is structured. In order to do this, using the Bible, locate the quotations from the references given. For example, the name given as the reference, say, Leviticus, gives you the book, which is like a chapter within the Bible. This is the first thing to look up. The 'Books' within the Bible were written by different people and this is why many are named after them. Next is the first number which gives you the chapter within the 'book'. Finally the number or numbers after the semi colon gives you the paragraph. Looking up references helps one to become au fait with the structure of the Bible, thus making it easier to follow later on when perhaps the time comes to read it all through. Incidentally, the quotations from the Bible have been chosen from the **Authorised Version**.

Parents and older children may enjoy the Natural History notes, kindly written by my friend and colleague Trevor Beer MBE, that relate not only to Biblical Lands but also to the British Isles as many wildlife species, particularly birds, have a wide distribution range. If you are planning a holiday perhaps check this book to see if you are likely to see some of the species mentioned.

Most importantly we must try to look after the flora and fauna in our own gardens and also in the churchyards, our own little 'Gardens of Eden'. I believe that is the right thing to do. Not only that, but if wild species are our indicator species, with people at the head of the food chain, then by protecting them we also protect our own race for the future. If we all pull together and do our bit for the Earth, no matter how small, even putting up a nest box or creating a wildlife pond, it will make a difference. All victories for Nature add up to create a much bigger picture. We need to look forward to a happy future so that future generations may have the same privileges as those we have enjoyed.

Peace & Light,
Endymion Beer.
www.naturama.co.uk

PART ONE

Introducing the Birds of the Bible

"The time of the singing of birds is come,
And the voice of the turtle is heard in our land;"
Song of Solomon 2:12

Reading the Bible at a young age can prove to be a daunting task for it is such a big book! As an ordinary British Citizen, and not an expert or scientist, my aim has been to bring the Bible closer to home. I felt there was no better way to achieve this than by celebrating the Wildlife of Bible.

Whilst the Holy Lands consist of much desert and includes the Red Sea, Dead Sea, Mediterranean and other famous waters, the land is vast and is altogether quite different to our own British terrain. Strange then, to find the familiar Barn Owl (Tyto alba) also living in the Bible Lands. In fact the reader may be surprised at just how many bird species there are in Biblical Lands that are familiar to us. Perhaps readers will relate better or feel closer to the Bible via our link with the wildlife. The bird section is my personal favourite, perhaps because I enjoy bird watching. Now there's an idea… a birds of the Bible field trip… such a shame Sunday Schools are dying out. My thanks to Trevor for writing the Natural History Notes that accompany all three sections to the book.

The Raven

And it came to pass at the end of forty days, that Noah opened the window of the ark which he had made:
*and he sent forth a **raven**, which went forth to and fro, until the waters were dried up from off the earth.* Genesis 8:6,7

*And it shall be, that thou shalt drink of the brook; and I have commanded the **ravens** to feed thee there.* I Kings 17:4

*Consider the **ravens**: for they neither sow nor reap; which neither have storehouse nor barn; and God feedeth them:...* St.Luke 12:24

Natural History Notes on the Raven. (Corvus corax)

The first bird mentioned in the Bible and the largest of the Crow family. One of the birds which Noah sent out during the floods it went 'forth and fro', until the waters from off the Earth dried up. The Raven is associated with myths and legends not only in Europe, but in North America and Asia and it is thought by some to be the totem bird of the 'Birdman' painting at Lascaux.

Biblically it is referred to in Genesis, the flood; and in the feeding of Elijah, as well as Isaiah 34:11, and Leviticus 1:15, and in the Book of Job, one suggestion, quite wrongly, that Ravens make bad parents. The Raven is a species with an unusually wide range. It covers the whole of the North American continent other than the S and E states of the USA. Northwards it is found up the coast of Greenland and north Canadian islands. It also ranges the whole European and Asiatic landmass from W to E and northwards above 70° line in Scandinavia and Siberia, and in Africa it covers all of the northern part above about 15°. This vast range extends over the bulk of the Northern Hemisphere from tropical deserts to high arctic cliffs and from sea level to 4480m in Eastern Tibet. (Vous, 1960)

The Raven
(Corvus corax)

In the British Isles it is widespread and resident with large numbers in Wales and South-West England holding a stable population. Their deep 'pruck pruck' calls as they fly overhead are a delight to hear. The Raven has suffered from man's persecution over the years but there are signs that our more enlightened attitudes and understanding is bringing about an increase in its numbers generally.

The Raven breeds and lays its eggs very early in the year, usually at traditional nest sites. The adults are very good parents during the 21 day incubation and five or six weeks to fledging. Only one brood is raised each year.

The word Raven remains almost unchanged since Anglo-Saxon times when it was Hrafn. Odin the Norse God was Hrafnagnd, the Raven God, who had two Ravens who flew all over the world then returned to tell him all that was happening.

There is a Brown-necked Raven (C.ruficollis) frequently seen in Biblical Lands.

Old country names include Corbie Craw in Scotland, Fiach, Ireland, and Marburan in Cornwall. The scientific name Corvus corax is from corvus (L) Raven and corax(GR) Raven.

The Dove

References to find:

*Also he (Noah) sent forth a **dove** from him, to see if the waters were abated from off the face of the ground;
but the **dove** found no rest for the sole of her foot, and she returned unto him into the ark,
for the waters were on the face of the whole earth: then he put forth his hand, and took her, and pulled her in unto him into the ark.*
Genesis 8:8,9

*And when the days of her purifying are fulfilled, for a son, or for a daughter, she shall bring a lamb of the first year for a burnt offering,
and a young **pigeon**, or a **turtledove**, for a sin offering, unto the door of the tabernacle of the congregation, unto the priest:*
Leviticus 12:6

*And he said unto him, Take me an heifer of three years old, and a she goat of three years old,
and a ram of three years old, and a **turtledove**, and a young **pigeon**. Genesis 15:9*

*And I said, Oh that I had wings like a **dove**! For then would I fly away, and be at rest. Psalm 55:6*

*Oh deliver not the soul of thy **turtledove** unto the multitude of the wicked: Psalm 74:19*

*O ye that dwell in Moab, leave the cities, and dwell in the rock,
and be like the **dove** that maketh her nest in the sides of the hole's mouth.*
Jeremiah 48:28

Natural History Notes on the Turtle Dove

The Turtle Dove (Streptopelia turtur) is a migratory species visiting the British Isles as a breeding bird during spring and summer. It has a wide breeding range in Europe and is found as far north as the southern Baltic Shores and North Sea. It winters in Africa.

It is a bird of open woodlands and usually feeds on the ground though it may be found nesting where trees remain in wet slack areas of coastal dunes. As with other pigeons it will drink salty as well as fresh water.

The turtle dove is a smallish, slender bird of about 11ins, (28cm) the adult having blue-grey head, neck, flanks and rump. The back and wings are red-brown with black centres to the feathers giving a mottled effect. There is a black and white striped patch on the side of the neck. The breast is pink, the abdomen and under tail coverts white. The tail is black with white edges and tip. The bill is black, the legs and eye rims red. Juveniles are duller and without the neck patch. The flight is straight and strong.

2 white eggs are laid in May or June and incubated by both adults for 13-14 days, the young vacating the nest at about 18 days. In the North the turtle dove is single brooded but elsewhere two broods are common.

Food is mostly plant food, mainly seeds of various kinds and the bird is not as reliant on grain gleanings as some references suggest. The usual call is a gentle purring 'rroorr, rroorr, rroorr,' usually repeated three times. It may also make a sharp clicking 'gopeck', not unlike the male red grouse mating call.

Our Lord referred to the dove as a symbol of simplicity and it became an emblem for the Holy Spirit. The dove is mentioned more often in the Bible than any other bird, over 50 times. It is first referred to in the story of the flood. (Genesis 8:8-12). There are a further 11 references to pigeons.

The two groups of species of doves, or pigeons are the genus Streptopelia which includes Turtle Dove and Collared Dove, and the genus Columba which includes the Wood Pigeon, Stock Dove and Rock Dove. All these are found in Bible Lands.

The Turtle Dove
(*Streptopelia turtur*)

The Collared Dove
(*Streptopelia decaocto*)

The Wood Pigeon (Columba palumbus) commonly seen as a wintering bird in areas such as the forests of Gilead, is also our own Wood Pigeon. It heads north in March.

The Collared Dove, (Streptopelia decaocto) of pink-buff colouring with a black neck collar is probably the commonest dove in Bible Lands. It has colonised Britain since the 1950s and is now numerous and widespread here in urban and suburban habitats as well as in farming country-side so is well known by all, as a 'garden' bird.

Streptopelia (GR) a necklace; decaocto (GR) a dove or wood pigeon.

Columba (L) a pigeon or dove; palumbus (L) a wood pigeon, a ring dove.

Turtur (L) a turtle dove.

The Wood Pigeon
(Columba palumbus)

The Cormorant

References to find:

*But the **cormorant** and the bittern shall possess it; the owl also and the raven shall dwell in it: and he shall stretch out upon it the line of confusion, and the stones of emptiness.*

Isaiah 34:11

*…and the hawk after his kind, and the little owl, and the **cormorant**… (Shall not be eaten)*

Leviticus 11:17

Natural History Notes on the Cormorant. (Phalacrocorax carbo)

Regarded as a common species of Bible Lands and a bird that is found almost everywhere in seas and inland waters of large size. In the British Isles the breeding range is much as that of the shag though in the N and W of Scotland and W of Ireland the latter bird predominates. Elsewhere the Cormorant tends to be more abundant. It is a large bulky, black looking bird of 36ins (90cm) and shows a purple-green sheen. The lower face and chin is white. The bill is yellowish, the legs black. A great deal of white at the breast and belly shows in immatures. The wing-beats are quick and strong and it may glide with still wings. On the water it swims low, holding the bill pointed up at an angle of about 45°.

Cormorants dive well and swim beneath the water using only the feet, moving in rapid jerks. It feeds exclusively on fish. Breeding is usually in colonies, large nests built on rocky islets, cliff ledges or in tall trees inland. Usually 3-4 eggs are laid in April to June and incubated by both adults for a month. The nestlings remain in the nest for about 7 weeks and fledge fully around the 8th week. They are completely independent at 3 months old.

The large wings of the cormorant are less well covered and protected by contour feathers than are those of most diving birds, thus they need to dry them following a spell of diving. It is also thought the cormorants feathers are less effectively waterproofed than most diving species hence our seeing the bird frequently standing with its wings held open.

As a species the cormorant inhabits Palaearctic, Indian, Ethiopian, E.Nearctic and Australasian regions. The typical race breeds in Iceland, Faroes, Norway, Finland and Murman coast to White Sea, and in N.America on coasts of Greenland, Gulf of St.Lawrence and Nova Scotia. Replaced by allied races in mid and S.Europe to China and Japan. Some wander S to S W Europe, N.Atlantic Coast of Africa and in America to Ontario, New York, Maryland and S.Carolina.

Referred to in Lev 11.17 and Deuteronomy 14.17, met with frequently on coasts, lakes and rivers of Palestine. P.desmarestii, a similar species is also found around the Mediterranean.

Phalacrocorax from phalakros (GR) bald headed, and korax (GR) korakos, a raven, anything hooked like a raven's bill. Cormorants have a sharp, hooked bill and usually part of the face is naked.

Old country names include Sea Crow, Coal Goose and Isle of Wight Parson. James I kept cormorants in a semi-domesticated state on the Thames at Westminster to catch fish and the Master of Cormorants was a member of the Royal Household.

The Cormorant
(*Phalacrocorax carbo*)

The Cuckoo

….and the night hawk, and the **cuckow***, and the hawk after his kind…. (Shall not be eaten)*
Deuteronomy 14:15

Natural History Notes on the Cuckoo

I find the cuckoo quite fascinating to contemplate in Biblical terms in that we know the **European Cuckoo (Cuculus canorus)** and the **Great Spotted Cuckoo (Clamator glandarius)** are found in Bible Lands.

Today's zoologists ponder on the possibility the translation of the Hebrew word 'Shalaf' is wrong and that some member of the gull family, Larus, is correct. However, if one considers, 'from their spittle grasshoppers are produced', and references to their 'short and small flight', the actual cuckoo wins my vote. Cuckoos commonly take grasshoppers and 'woolly bear' caterpillars and to the casual observer may well be 'producing' them in their spittle.

Even the reference in Lev 11:13-16 and Deut 14:15, which says, 'and the cuckoo and the hawk after his kind', has me thinking of our British and European Cuckoo. Any keen nature watcher will know how like the sparrowhawk a cuckoo is when it hedgehops across the countryside and many today, even with binoculars to the ready, mistake the one for the other.

The Cuckoo (*Cuculus canorus*)

And why a forbidden bird? It must be the cuckoo who lays its eggs in the nests of other species, ousting the young in order that the host species raises its own. The Bible is full of such righteous symbolism and gulls to my mind, would not rouse the same ire.

The cuckoo has a magic all its own. What other bird has the public writing to newspapers about its arrival in the British springtime? The chiff chaffs and willow warblers certainly don't yet the former heralds the spring before the cuckoo every year!

Consider, too, how some cuckoos virtually match the colours of host species eggs with their own and we have Meadow Pipit Cuckoos, Dunnock Cuckoos and Reed Warbler Cuckoos for example. Utterly fascinating.

Cuculus (L) the cuckoo; canorus (L) melodious, sweet sounding.

The House Sparrow
(Passer domesticus)

The Sparrow

References to find:

*Yea, the **sparrow** hath found an house,
And the swallow a nest for herself, where she may lay her young.*
Psalm 84:3

*I watch, and am
As a **sparrow** alone upon the house top.* Psalm 102:7

*Fear ye not therefore, ye are of more value than many **sparrows**.*
St. Matthew 10:31

Natural History Notes on the Sparrow

The sparrow occurs many times in the Bible including references by Jesus Christ Himself. We know our own British **House Sparrow (Passer domesticus)** is found in Biblical Lands so is it he referred to in Psalm 102:7 'I watch and am as a sparrow alone upon the house top'?

This is how we see the cock sparrow during the breeding season as he watches, chirping, over his mate, nest, eggs and young. In Britain it is present all year and generally found near human habitations. They seldom fly far from their birthplace and most populations around the world are sedentary.

Both sexes build the nest of dried grass in a hole in building or tree or sometimes in hedgerows where the nest is then domed. 3-5 eggs are usually laid April-August with incubation being 12-14 days, mainly by the female. Young are fed by both parents and fly at about 15 days. Up to three broods may be raised in a year. Food is grain and weed seeds, insects and their larvae. Comes readily to bird tables for scraps.

The Tree Sparrow
(Passer montanus)

The name Sparrow is from the Anglo Saxon spearwa and old country names include Spadger, Spurgie, Lum Lintie, Cuddy and Thatch Sparrow.

Passer (L) a sparrow; and domesticus, domus (L) a house, domesticus (L) belonging to the house.

The Tree Sparrow (P.montanus) is not restricted to mountainous areas as its 'montanus' name suggests. It is found in Britain and Europe, Asia including India, south to the Burma-Vietnam area, Indonesia and East to Japan. It is favourite with some naturalists as the sparrow of Scripture.

NightHawk

Reference to find:

*…and the owl, and the **night hawk**, and the cuckow…. (Shall not be eaten)*
Leviticus 11:16

Natural History Notes on the Nighthawk

So many of the birds in the Bible were 'in abomination' and the nighthawk is yet another of those. It is almost certainly a reference to the **Nightjar (Caprimulgus europaeus)** which winters in Africa and passes through Biblical Lands in summer time.

It is 'our' Nightjar, too, of course, the summer visitor we love to see at sunset and moonrise times flying about its territory like a gigantic moth, wing clapping and churring into the night.

Caprimulgus (GR) means goat-sucker and an old belief which dates back at least to Aristotle tells us the bird would take milk from goat's udders at night. It doesn't, but such is the magic of folklore.

In Britain it is a May to October visitor which nests in an unlined scrape on the ground, often near dead wood. Two eggs are laid in May to July and incubated mainly by the female for about 18 days. Young are fed by both adults. They leave the nest after about 7 days but stay close by and fly after about 17 days. Usually two broods are raised.

Food is insects mainly caught in flight in the wide open gape of the bird as it flies about, twisting and turning in twilight and moonlight. The strange churring call is issued as the bird lies along a tree branch, often turning its head from side to side as it does so. Numbers have been decreasing for some years. It winters mainly in Africa, from the Sudan to Cape Province.

Old country names include Evejar, Heath Jar, Night Hawk, Moth Hawk, Goat Sucker, Goat Owl, Fern Owl and Flying Toad.

The Nightjar (*Caprimulgus europaeus*)

The Quail

References to find:

*And it came to pass, that at even the **quails** came up, and covered the camp: and in the morning the dew lay round about the host.*
Exodus 16:13

*And there went forth a wind from the Lord, and brought **quails** from the sea, and let them fall by the camp, as it were a day's journey on this side, and as it were a day's journey on the other side, round about the camp, and as it were two cubits high upon the face of the earth. And the people stood up all that day, and all that night, and all the next day, and they gathered the **quails:***
Numbers 11:31,32

Natural History Notes on the Quail

So abundant years ago that the tiny bird migrated in swarms and was known to literally crowd onto ships and apparently put them in danger of sinking! The **Quail (Coturnix coturnix)** is still common in Bible Lands as a common passage migrant but the species has become rare in Britain. The Quail is the smallest of the European game birds. Only 7in (17.5cms) long the stocky little bird has been shot and netted in Britain as a game bird and delicacy but no doubt the constant netting of many thousands of quail as they rest on the southern coasts of Africa on migration, has caused a marked decline in numbers. Quail tend to migrate at night, a point noted in Exodus.

The Quail
(*Coturnix coturnix*)

In Britain the Quail is a farmland bird found mainly in crop fields where it feeds on seeds of grasses and weeds, with some snails and caterpillars taken. They arrive here in May, remaining to October as a summer visitor and breeding bird. The female makes a scrape in the ground among crops or grasses and lines it sparsely with grass or leaves. She lays in late May or June, usually 7-12 eggs, and incubates these for 18-21 days. The young leave the nest after a few hours, tended by the female, and begin to fly at 11-12 days.

Old country names include Wet-my-feet, Wet-my-lips, and Quick-me-dick from its call notes, Quailzie in Scotland and Rine in Cornwall. The Latin coturnix simply means a Quail.

According to classical Greek writers, the flesh of the quail was made unwholesome by the bird's eating poisonous plants such as Hellebore.

The Partridge

References to find:

*As the **partridge** sitteth on eggs, and hatcheth them not; so he that getteth riches,*
and not by right, shall leave them in the midst of his days, and at his end shall be a fool.

I Samuel 17:11

Now therefore, let not my blood fall to the earth before the face of the Lord: for the king of Israel
*is come out to seek a flea, as when one doth hunt a **partridge** in the mountains.*

I Samuel 26:20

Natural History Notes on the Partridge

Looking at World distribution maps of birds the likeliest candidate for the partridge of Bible Lands is the **Desert Partridge (Ammoperdix leyi)** also known as the **Sand Partridge**. It is a small bird twixt a quail and a Grey Partridge in size and is still common in Bible Lands. There is a white mark in front of both eyes. The larger **Chukar Partridge (Alectoris chukar)** and which has typical black and white flank barring is also found at the edges of deserts in Biblical regions.

The Chukar Partridge
(Alectoris chukar)

The British native partridge **(Perdix perdix)** is known as the **Grey Partridge** but so many have been imported from central Europe that it is difficult to be sure of the origin of those we see. It has even been tagged 'the Hungarian partridge' by some which reflects well the import aspect. Our bird is present all year though declines have been notable over the past decade and we see more of the red-legged or French partridge these days. It is a sedentary species.

They prefer farmland for nesting, arable or grassland with good cover from hedges, shrubs, ditches, and may be found in coastal sand dunes and moorland edges. The female makes a scrape, lines it with dried grass and leaves and lays 12-18 eggs in late April or May. Incubation, by the female only is about 24 days. Young run about a few hours after hatching, tended by both adults, and fly after about 2 weeks. Partridges feed mainly on grain, buds, flowers, leaves and seeds of low growing plants. They will also take insects, spiders, snails and slugs. When roosting together in a group, or covey, they face outwards to watch for predators.

Perdix (L) a partridge. Inhabits Europe including the British Isles, Southern Scandinavia, Northern Spain, and ranging across Europe to Asia Minor and Central Asia.

Old Country names include Girgirick, Grey Bird, Stumpey and English Partridge.

The Partridge *(Perdix perdix)*

Chickens – Cock & Hen

*Jesus said unto him, Verily I say unto thee, That this night, before the **cock crow**, thou shalt deny me thrice.*
St.Matthew 26:34

*Watch ye therefore: for ye know not when the master of the house cometh, at even, or at midnight,
or at the **cockcrowing**, or in the morning: lest coming suddenly he find you sleeping.*
Mark 13:35

*O Jerusalem, Jerusalem, thou that killest the prophets, and stonest them which are sent unto thee, how often would
I have gathered thy children together, even as a hen gathereth her **chickens** under her wings, and, ye would not!*
St.Matthew 23:37

Rhode Island Red

Natural History Notes on Chickens, Cock & Hen

Jesus refers to the 'cock crowing' as at midnight or in the morning and I feel we can take it from that He is close to our own dawn-time cock crowing, and cocks do crow first in the early darkness hours. It was a cock who praised God with seven hymns according to Hebrew Legend.

When poultry were first imported to Bible Lands is not known, though Solomon's household provisions included 'fatted fowl', but whether they were chickens, geese, swans or whatever is mere conjecture.

That the cock crowed and still crows as a natural measure of time is certain enough. Similarly the hen and her chicks are referred to by Jesus in the New Testament, in Matthew and Luke.

Hoopoe

Reference to find:

*….and the stork, the heron after her kind, and the **lapwing**, and the bat. (Shall not be eaten)*
Leviticus 11:19

Natural History Notes on The Hoopoe

Referred to in the Authorised, or King James Version of the Bible as 'Lapwing' it seems certain that the bird referred to in Leviticus (11.:19) is the **Hoopoe (Upupa epops)**. Sacred to the Egyptians and thus 'unclean' to the Hebrews, legend has it the Hoopoe received its beautiful crest from Solomon for sheltering him in the desert. The bird also carried an invitation to the Queen of Sheba, from Solomon, inviting her to visit him. More like a homing pigeon!

The Hoopoe breeds in the northern Bible Lands and over winters in Africa. It is increasingly recorded in Britain as a rare spring vagrant but it does nest here occasionally.

A bird such as the Hoopoe, flying 3,000 miles north from Africa may well make an error of judgment and overshoot its breeding grounds. The Hoopoe, heading for Brittany, overshoots the English Channel to end up with us. Southerly winds often 'aid' the overshoot which may relate mainly to less experienced birds in the first summer and thus on their first migration northwards. Only northern birds migrate; European birds winter in Africa, south of the Sahara. They usually nest in places with scattered trees, perhaps in an old willow or crevice in a farm building. Hoopoes do not keep their nest site clean and Arabs disapprove of them as unclean feeders on dunghills. 5-8 eggs are laid with incubation by the female only for about 18 days. Young are fed by both parents and leave after 3-4 weeks. Food is mainly beetle grubs, grasshoppers, moths, ants, earwigs, flies, woodlice, spiders and such. The bird is 11.5ins (28cms).

The Hoopoe
(Upupa epops)

Upupa (L) a hoopoe; epops (GR) a hoopoe. Named from its call.

The Lapwing *(Vanellus vanellus)* or Green Plover as we know it in the British Isles. Yet not the 'lapwing' of Biblical scripture.

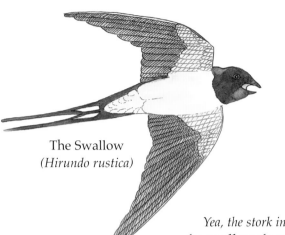

The Swallow
(Hirundo rustica)

Swallow

References to find:

*As the bird by wandering, as the **swallow** by flying,*
Proverbs 26:2

*Yea, the stork in the heaven knoweth her appointed times; and the turtle and the crane and
the **swallow** observe the time of their coming; but my people know not the judgment of the Lord.*
Jeremiah 8:7

Natural History Notes on the Swallow

Who does not look out for the swallow each year, a bird synonymous with Springtime and this applies also to the Bible Lands (Jeremiah) as is their constant chattering, (Isaiah). The **Swallow (Hirundo rustica)** remains a common migrant of Biblical Lands, nesting in and about human habitation whenever it is found.

There have been some who feel the Swift and House Martin might be the birds referred to by the Hebrew word Deror but modern scholars seem to be agreed the Swallow is the species meant. Deror simply means liberty so in translation the swallow was chosen as the 'bird of freedom' and marvelled at for its ability to fly away and return each year, even to the same nest site as previously.

Swifts In Flight *(Apus apus)*

As to the Swift there was some argument as to the translation of Sis, with writers suggesting it is the Crane but it makes more sense that it is the swift. Isaiah, in Hezekiah's sickness period refers to him chattering like a crane (Sis) or a swallow, though the Septuagint says sis is 'Chelidon' or swallow. The two species are always linked whereas Crane seems unlikely. No doubt the arguments will continue but some species of swift seems likeliest for sis.

Our Swallow is 7½ ins (18cms) long and well known by all who love birds. It is migratory, with us from March to October, our birds wintering in S.Africa, others wintering in tropical S.America, Africa and S and S.E Asia.

24

Both sexes build saucer shaped nests of mud and dried grasses lined with feathers, usually on a ledge or beam in a building. Eggs are laid in May-August and incubated by the female for about 15 days. Young are fed by both adults and leave after 18-21 days. Food is flying insects. Country names include Barn Swallow, Chimney Swallow and Red Fronted Swallow.

Hirundo (L) a swallow; rusticus (L) belonging to the countryside, rural.

Heron

Reference to find:

*….and the cormorant, and the stork, and the **heron** after her kind,…. (Shall not be eaten)*
Deuteronomy 14:18

Natural History Notes on the Heron

Leviticus (11.13-19) refers to 'the heron after her kind', as being unclean and clearly takes in the various herons and egrets seen in Biblical lands. Oddly the heron was considered to neglect its young, which the **Grey Heron (Ardea cinerea)** does not do in this writer's experience.

In Bible Lands the Grey Heron, the **Purple Heron (Ardea purpurea)** and **Night Heron (Nycticorax nycticorax)** are commonly seen along with 7 other species. All are migrants found anywhere where they can obtain their diet of fish, mice, rats, water voles and waterfowl.

Where there are sizable trees the heron will nest high in their branches, otherwise they will nest on the ground. It is a large bird of 36ins (90cms) but not heavy. Nesting is usually colonial, some heronries being very old, traditional sites. The female arranges the platform of sticks or reeds brought by the male and nests may be 2m across. Eggs are laid from Feb-May, usually early in spring and 3-5 is the usual number. Incubation, shared by both adults, is about 25 days. Young are fed by both adults, the young fledging after 7-8 weeks. The heron is a resident species here but in winter some may move to coasts and a few migrants may arrive from northern Europe.

The Grey Heron
(Ardea cinerea)

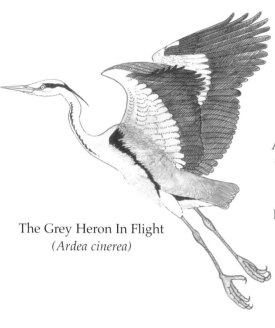

The Grey Heron In Flight
(Ardea cinerea)

Old country names include Harn, Ern, Long Necky and Longie Crane. Young are known as Branchers. The Old English was Hragra, the name Hegrie still in use in the Shetlands.

Ardea, L, a heron; and cinerea, from cinereus (L) ash-coloured. Of interest, as with the Collared Dove, the Little Egret (Egretta garzetta) has recently begun to colonise Britain, from the continent and now breeds in several counties.

Egret from Aigrette (FR) a tuft of feathers or plume, an egret. Garzetta, garza (IT) an egret.

The Purple Heron breeds in Holland and occasionally visits Britain on migration.

Bittern

References to find:

*I will also make it a possession for the **bittern**, and pools of water:* Isaiah 14.23

*And flocks shall lie down in the midst of her, all the beasts of the nations: both the cormorant and the **bittern** shall lodge in the upper lintels of it; their voice shall sing in the windows; desolation shall be in the thresholds: for he shall uncover the cedar work.*

Zephaniah 2:14

Bittern
(Botaurus stellaris)

Natural History Notes on the Bittern

According to some translators the Bittern of the Bible is the Syrian hedgehog, but the Isaiah 14:23 reference 'I will also make it a possession for the Bittern, and pools of water' suggests the **Bittern (Botaurus stellaris)** of the Heron family, even against the modern's favourite choice the Owl.

Though not a small bird its beautiful plumage camouflages it so well in its reeded haunts it is difficult to observe. I have found it on occasions in Britain in harsh winters and even when watching it, often had to rub my eyes and find it all over again - in the same spot!

The Bittern feeds on eels, earthworms, frogs, voles and mice and even the young of other ground or reedbed nesting birds in the breeding season.

Sparrowhawk
(Accipiter nisus)

Hawk

Reference to find:

*Doth the **hawk** fly by thy wisdom,
And stretch her wings toward the south?* Job 39:26

Natural History Notes on the Hawk

Methinks it would be wrong to do other than leave the term 'hawk' to cover diurnal raptors such as the peregrine and sparrowhawk, rather than point to one species only. Thus 'hawk' in the Bible includes the hawks proper and the various falcons probably though the comments therein are scant enough.

'The hawk after his kind' of Leviticus and Deuteronomy encompasses a number of species surely and the reference in Job, 'Doth the hawk fly by thy wisdom and stretch her wings towards the South' suggests a goodly knowledge of migration in birds.

In Bible Lands the **Sparrowhawk (Accipiter nisus)** is a winter visitor and passage migrant and is the Sparrowhawk we in Britain all know so well. The **Goshawk (Accipiter gentilis)** is scarcer and recorded as a straggler, whilst the little **Shikra (A.badius)** is a passage migrant from the Southern Caspian region and not seen here.

Goshawk
(Accipiter gentilis)

Of course 'our' sparrowhawk is present all year and most populations are sedentary but northern birds winter just south of their breeding range. Males are 11ins (28cms) and females 15ins (37.5cms).

Twig nests are built in trees, often by the female alone, with eggs usually laid in May and numbering 4-6. Incubation is by the female alone for about 35 days, the male catching and bringing food to her. Young are tended by both adults and fledge at around 24-30 days. Food is small birds, the larger female capable of taking birds to the size of wood pigeons. Occasionally mice, voles, young rabbits and insects are eaten.

Old country names include Blue Hawk, Pigeon Hawk, Spar Hawk and Stannin Hawk.

Accipiter (L) the Common Hawk; niscus, King of Megara according to Greek legend, who was changed into a white sparrowhawk. Widespread and common in Britain and Europe, Africa, east to Japan, including India, Burma, Vietnam and Indonesia.

Osprey
(Pandion haliaetus)

Osprey

Reference to find:

*And these are they which ye shall have in abomination among the fowls; they shall not be eaten, they are an abomination: the eagle, and the ossifrage and the **ospray** and the vulture…* Leviticus 11:13,14

Natural History Notes on the Osprey (Pandion haliaetus)

As the Osprey (ospray) is mentioned specifically (Deut XIV.12) and is found in Bible Lands albeit not commonly, preferring the seashore and the rivers of the coast, it is said to avoid the Sea of Galilee. (Wood, 1887). Also known as the Fish Eagle, the Osprey has done well in recent years in Britain, particularly in Scotland where the bird is very much a part of tourism. It is also observed in England on its Spring and Autumn migration to and from its breeding grounds.

Pandion, the legendary King of Athens, and haliaeetos (L) the osprey or sea eagle.

Kestrel

Reference to find:

*…Doth the **hawk** fly by thy wisdom, And stretch her wings toward the south?* Job 39:26

Natural History Notes on the Kestrel (Falco tinnunculus)

Said to be the commonest of the smaller raptors of the Bible Lands this is the same species we know so well in Britain as the Wind-hover. It is a falcon, not a true hawk but is undoubtedly lumped in with the term Netz, or hawk, deemed the correct translation.

Falco, falx (L) genitive falcis, a sickle, a reference to the curved talons and or wing shape of falcons; and tinnunculus, tinnio (L) I ring or tinkle, and tinnulus (L) ringing, tinkling. The little bell ringer, referring to the rapid high pitched call.

Kestrel
(Falco tinnunculus)

Glede

Reference to find:

*…ye shall not eat: the eagle, and the ossifrage, and the ospray, and the **glede**, and the **kite** and the vulture after his kind,*
Deuteronomy 14:12,13

Natural History Notes on the Glede

The Authorised or King James version of the Bible is the only one to refer to the Glede, which in England and Scotland is an old name for the Red Kite, and in northern Scotland, a name for the **Buzzard (Buteo buteo).** Gled and Glead are other spellings, the word referring to the gliding flight of these birds. Interestingly the Marsh Harrier is known as the Bog Gled in parts of Scotland, a glider of the bog.

Buzzard *(Buteo buteo)*

Red Kite
(Milvus milvus)

Kites are basically scavengers, preferring carrion to having to hunt. Nature has designed them thus, weaker of foot and talon compared to most raptors and catching only small mammals and a few birds otherwise. In Britain their stronghold is in Wales, with some introductions in recent years, to our Red Kite population. There are no Black Kites breeding in Britain today.

Red Kite (Milvus milvus) Milvus (L) a bird of prey, a kite.

Black Kite (M.Migrans) migrans, migro (L) I move from place to place; migrans, wandering.

Encountered almost all over warmer areas of the Old World, northern populations migrating south in winter, this includes the Bible Lands and we should hold to the red kite in the Bible context.

Black Kite *(Milvus migrans)*

Note: Compare the straight rear edge of the Black Kite's spread tail to the ever present fork of the Red Kite's in flight.

The Owl

I am a brother to dragons,
*And a companion to **owls**.* Job 30:29

But wild beasts of the desert shall lie there; and their houses shall be full of doleful creatures;
*and **owls** shall dwell there, and satyrs shall dance there.* Isaiah 13.21

*…the **little owl**, and the comorant, and the great owl, and the swan, and the pelican,…. (Shall not be eaten)* Leviticus 11:17,18

And thorns shall come up in her palaces, nettles and brambles in the fortresses there-of:
*and it shall be an habitation of dragons, and a court for **owls**.* Isaiah 34:13

Natural History Notes on Owls

A great deal of speculation surrounds the Owls of the Bible but the likeliest two that we know inhabit Bible Lands and many other countries including Britain and Europe are the Little Owl and the Barn or Screech Owl. Indeed translations of Lev. 11:16, 17, refer to the 'Little Owl' along with other birds, and there is no logical reason not to consider it and the Barn owl as 'meant' so to speak.

The **Little Owl (Athene noctua)** is the bird of wisdom of Athene the Goddess of Wisdom, a bird revered in Greek history, the 'wise old owl' of the country-side that has a liking for village life and certain types of buildings, as indeed does the Barn Owl.

Only 8½ ins (22cms) the Little owl was introduced into Britain from the Continent towards the end of the 19th Century and it spread rapidly. It is a diurnal owl, hunting mainly at dawn and dusk. It often perches near its nest site on posts or telegraph wires bobbing away and wagging its tail if approached. The flight is conspicuously undulating, the usual call note a plaintive 'kiew-kiew'. Present all year with a preference for light wooded farmland and coastal dune areas. The Little Owl nests in tree holes, burrows, walls, buildings, quarries and such, using no nest material. Usually lays 3-5

The Barn Owl
(Tyto alba)

eggs, the female incubating them for about 28 days. Young are fed by both adults and fly after about 5 weeks. Food is mainly insects, voles, mice, young rats and other small mammals.

Athene from Pallas Athene, Goddess of Wisdom; and noctua (L) a night owl.

The Barn Owl (Tyto alba) is the Screech Owl or White Owl, present all year in Britain and mainly sedentary though birds from Central Europe disperse over considerable distances. It is 13½ins (34cms) and in silent flight shows the white undersides of its wings.

The Barn Owl does not build a nest and eggs are often laid on disgorged pellets. Sites include old buildings, ruins, hollow trees, quarries, corn ricks and nest boxes. The main egg laying period is April and May with 4-6 eggs laid and incubated by the female for about 33 days. Young are fed by both adults and fly after 9-12 weeks. Two broods are fairly common.

Food is rats, mice, voles, shrews, moles, small birds, beetles and moths. Sometimes bats and fish are taken. Barn Owls may be seen hunting by day when food is scarce, or they have young to feed.

Tyto, from tuto (GR) a night owl; and alba (L) white.

The Little Owl
(Athene noctua)

Eagle

References to find:

*Doth the **eagle** mount up at thy command,*
And make her nest on high? Job 39:27

Golden Eagle's Head
(Aquila chrysaetos)

Natural History Notes on Eagles

It seems that references to Eagles in the Scriptures, according to modern ornithologists, possibly refer to the Griffon Vulture. However, we know today that the **Golden Eagle (Aquila chrysaetos)** does visit the Bible Lands and may have done so more frequently in the past.

The eagles in Bible Lands today are mainly migrants and over wintering birds. The **Bonelli's Eagle (Hieraaetus fasciatus)** is seen there as is the smaller **Short-toed Eagle (Circaetus gallicus)** also known as the **Snake Eagle.** Even the **Imperial Eagle (Aquila heliaca)** is a winter visitor and a bird of passage from S.E.Europe so let us stay with eagles, if that is what the Bible says.

Our own Golden Eagle is so majestic with its 7ft (2.5m) wing span and is capable of 90mph hunting speeds in pursuit of its prey. Males are about 30ins (75cms) females 35ins (88cms) and in Britain, seem to be doing well currently. Eagles mate for life and usually have two or three eyries which they use in rotation.

Enormous stick nests are made and added to annually, being repaired before the breeding season and often decorated with greenery in the manner of Buzzards. Both sexes repair the nest in November or December and usually 2 eggs are laid in March or April. Incubation is mainly by the female for 40 days or so, the young being fed by both parents for about 12 weeks before they leave the nest.

Food is hares, grouse, some lambs and carrion. Golden Eagles are known to 'drive' deer over precipitous ledges to kill them, then eat them. Most sheep or lambs eaten are already dead and not killed by the Eagles.

Present all year the Golden Eagle now nests in England and Ireland as well as in its Scottish strongholds. Sedentary it survives in Europe in rugged mountain country.

Eagle symbolism comes from the Middle East via the Mediterranean, with eagle gods in Babylon and from the area around the Tigris and Euphrates. Coins dated to around 400BC in the Greek city of Elis have Eagles on them. 'Eagle-marrow' was sold as a cure for several ailments years ago, a huge scam as birds have hollow bones of course.

Aquila (L) an Eagle; chrysaetos from khrusos (GR) gold and aetos (GR) an Eagle. Inhabits North America, South to Mexico, Eurasia including Scandinavia and Scotland, England, Wales and Ireland, ranging South to Northern Africa, East to Arabia, India, Burma and Vietnam. As widespread as its wonderful wings.

Bonelli's Eagle
(*Hieraaetus fasciatus*)
Note: This Eagle is not resident
in the British Isles & is scarce.
Let us hope the species
does not die out.

Vulture

References to find:

*There is a path which no fowl knoweth, And which the **vulture's** eye hath not seen:* Job 28:7

*There shall the great owl make her nest, and lay, and hatch, and gather under her shadow:
there shall the **vultures** also be gathered, every one with her mate.* Isaiah 34:15

Natural History Notes on Vultures

A well established and frequently seen bird of Bible Lands is the **Griffon Vulture (Gyps fulvus)** recognised by its pale colour and darkly contrasting wing feathers.

The **Lammergeier** or **Bearded Vulture (Gypeatus barbatus)** tends to hold to its mountain fastnesses and is the well known 'Bone Breaker' who drops bones from a great height onto rocks in order to break them and eat them more easily. It is the **Ossifrage** of the Bible, Latin for 'Bone Breaker' and is the largest of the Bible Lands vultures being some 4ft (120cms) in length. It is resident but not common.

Other vultures include the breeding **Lappet-faced Vulture (Torgos tracheliotus)** and the passage migrant **Black Vulture (Aegypius monachus).** An often seen summer migrant is the smallest, the **Egyptian Vulture (Neophron percnopterus)** with its easily recognisable black and white plumage.

The Griffon Vulture
(Gyps fulvus)

Peacock

References to find:

*For the king had at sea a navy of Tharshish with the navy of Hiram:
once in three years came the navy of Tharshish, bringing gold, and silver, ivory, and apes, and **peacocks.*** I Kings 10.22

*Gavest thou the goodly wings unto the **peacocks***? Job 39:13

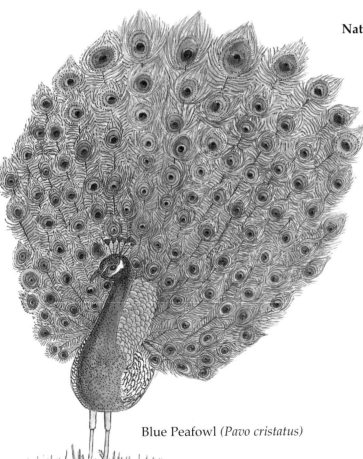

Natural History Notes on the Peacock

It is said Solomon imported the peacock to Bible Lands, and peahens too one imagines. Both the Kings I, and Job refer to peacocks, though modern translations state the reference in Job is actually to the Ostrich.

In Britain when we refer to Peacocks we mean the **Blue Peafowl (Pavo cristatus)** from India, now common on many estates and ornamental gardens and undoubtedly that which Solomon found he must have as part of his own glorious household.

Blue Peafowl (*Pavo cristatus*)

Ostrich

Reference to find:

Gavest thou the goodly wings unto the peacocks?
*Or wings and feathers unto the **ostrich**?*
Which leaveth her eggs in the earth,
And warmeth them in dust,
And forgetteth that the foot may crush them.
Job 39:13,14,15.

Natural History Notes on the Ostrich

Evidently the wild Ostrich of Bible Lands was a sub species **(Struthio camelus camelus)** and smaller than those we know in Africa. It is thought they became extinct following floods in S.Jordan as recently as 1966.

Pelican

Reference to find:

*I am like a **pelican** of the wilderness:*
I am like an owl of the desert. Psalm 102:6

Natural History Notes on the Pelican

Commonly seen in great flocks on migration twixt the Black Sea and their wintering quarters on the lakes of Uganda is the **White Pelican (Pelecanus onocrotalus)** a frequent migrant of Bible lands.

The White Pelican
(Pelecanus onocrotalus)

The Stork

Where the birds make their nests:
*As for the **stork**, the fir trees are her house.* Psalm 104:17

Then lifted I up mine eyes, and looked, and, behold, there came out two women, and the wind was in their wings;
*for they had wings like the wings of a **stork**: and they lifted up the ephah between the earth and the heaven.* Zechariah 5:9

Natural History Notes on the Stork

Two storks are found in Bible Lands today, the **White Stork (Ciconia ciconia)** a common passage migrant which occasionally over winters, and the **Black Stork (C.nigra)** a rarer species which is also a passage migrant that may over winter.

The White Stork
(Ciconia ciconia)

White Stork Flying
(Ciconia ciconia)

The Crane

References to find:

*Like a **crane** or a swallow, so did I chatter:* Isaiah 38:14

*Yea the Stork in the heaven knoweth her appointed times; and the turtle and the **crane** and the swallow observe the time of their coming;*
Jeremiah 8:7

Natural History Notes on the Crane

The Crane is referred to as 'a chatterer' in the Bible and the Hebrew word Aqur has been positively identified by zoologists as the genus Grus, the Crane. It has an unusual, distinctive call and the **Common Crane (Grus grus)** is a seasonal migrant to Bible lands. Huge numbers on migration would have been seen and heard as the great birds flew south for Africa's warmth from their northern European breeding grounds.

Cranes inhabit wetlands living on a wide variety of food including insects, small mammals, grasses and grain.

These days the Common Crane's status is that of a winter visitor, observed mainly in January migrating north in large numbers.

The Common Crane (*Grus grus*)

The Swan

Reference to find:

…and the great owl, and the **swan,** *and the pelican, and the gier eagle,…. (Shall not be eaten.)* Leviticus 11:18

Bewick's Swan (Head)
(Cygnus bewickii)

Whooper Swan (Head)
(Cygnus cygnus)

Mute Swan (Head)
(Cygnus olor)

Natural History Notes on the Swan

Mentioned in Leviticus and Deuteronomy but today said to be a total error in translation. The Mute, Bewick's and Whooper Swan have all been recorded in Bible Lands in fairly recent times but are extremely rare. Impossible to identify sadly.

Ibis.
The difficulty with 'swan' seems never to have been properly resolved and it makes no sense for it to have been included in the 'unclean' species of the law of Moses. The Ibis has been suggested and this would surely be the **Sacred Ibis (Threskiornis aethiopica)** much revered by ancient Egyptians. Some were mummified and preserved for over 3000 years. The bird is white. The other possible species is the **Glossy Ibis (Plegadis falcinellus)** and the Bible mentions 'black' which fits with this bird in some lights though it does show as having the deepest green plumage which can even light purple, blue and gold just as in our magpie.

Both species have been seen in Britain. I have photographed the Sacred Ibis in North Devon where one stayed for about 3 years and also found a Glossy Ibis in the same marshes some years later. Interestingly the Sacred Ibis is the emblem of the British Ornithologist's Union (BOU) and The Ibis is the title of their learned Journal.

Glossy Ibis *(Plegadis falcinellus)*

PART TWO

An Introduction to the
Other Animals of the Bible

"All things bright and beautiful,
All Creatures great and small…"
From Mrs Cecil Frances Alexander's Hymns For Little Children (1848)

In this second section of "A Celebration of Flora and Fauna of the Bible", readers will notice that I have occasionally illustrated the 'cousin' of a species found in Bible Lands, but all is explained in my colleague's Natural History Notes as we attempt to bring the Bible closer to home. It is good to know that in a way, we are not so far removed from the Holy Land, here in Britain, as we are linked by some of the animals we are all familiar with, and with other animals that walked our terrain long ago, such as the wolf for example. At the beginning, land masses were not divided in the way we know them to be today, so wildlife back then would have had free reign. Gone now are the behemoths, leviathans, satyrs and unicorns…..

With the selected quotations from the Bible, I have tried to be as varied as possible in including as many 'books' and chapters as I could to make looking up the references more interesting and diverse. I hope they will aid youngsters with their Bible study. My dream is that other religions around the world will follow suit and celebrate the wildlife of their holy scriptures. It is time the emphasis of our beliefs were at peace globally…..

Extraordinary Beasts
The Leviathan, Behemoth & The Unicorn

Cryptozoology may seem a fairly new science, the 'hidden' weird creatures unrecognised
so untagged by scientists, but the next four defy our searching and remain enigmas.

Artist's impression of The Leviathan

Leviathan

Reference to find:

There go the ships:
*There is that **leviathan,***
who thou hast made to play therein.
Psalm 104:26

Natural History Notes on The Leviathan

Four Old Testament references tell of this huge, monstrous creature that was God's play animal
at the end of busy days. Yet it could be 'controlled' by the Stickleback! Eventually the male was
slain, for God had already killed the female of the pair he had created in case, together, they
destroyed the Earth. Then there were none.

Some zoologists liken Leviathan to a gigantic crocodile. Fair enough, who but God Himself
would sport with such creatures? Once common in Egypt and revered as an emblem of the
pharaohs they have been hunted to extinction in Bible Lands and are no longer found in the wild.

However, only two? Created by God as his playthings? That does not fit with crocodiles and the
story of how the two died, so the species becoming extinct at God's hand, does not fit either. Two
enormous aquatic or semi aquatic creatures suddenly there and as suddenly gone.

Behemoth

Reference to find:

*Behold now **behemoth**, which I made with thee;*
He eateth grass as an ox.
Lo now, his strength is in his loins,
And his force is in the navel of his belly.
He moveth his tail like a cedar:

Job 40:15,16,17

Natural History Notes on the Behemoth

More of a land animal whereas Leviathan is a water creature. The two together God's greatest live animal creations. Having created them, God took away the male's desire to mate with the female, in order to prevent the species dominating the Earth. Seems as if He was experimenting and He didn't always get it right.

Again zoologists suggest Crocodile, Hippopotamus, and Elephant, as candidates but as both the Leviathan and the Behemoth could drink the Jordan dry, methinks these animals were one-offs as species and not creatures actually known by mankind.

Of course, we must remember there really were huge beasts, dinosaurs, mammoths, pleisiosaurs and such around and about long before mankind. Fossil evidence proves they were real and far better fit the stories.

I believe the Leviathan and Behemoth existed and were prehistoric 'monsters', perhaps the fore runners of dinosaurs of land and water that died 'at God's hand' before an opportunity to reproduce occurred. Part of Creation but not of Evolution shall we say. There must have been many such….

Artist's impression of The Behemoth

Unicorn

A Unicorn

Reference to find:

Will the unicorn be willing to serve thee,
Or abide by thy crib?
*Canst thou bind the **unicorn** with his band in the furrow?*
Or will he harrow the valleys after thee?

Job 39:9,10

Natural History Notes on the Unicorn

At least 9 references to the unicorn, a fabulous creature of great strength and purity. Sadly all have been changed to the 'wild ox' in modern translations. However the unicorn has come down through the ages and is here to stay, with its single horn on its brow.

The Aurochs, a wild ox, Bos primigenius, is the probable ancestor of domestic cattle. It is now extinct but was certainly known in Europe up to the 16th century.

Bos (L) an ox; primigenus (L) original, primitive.

Satyr

Reference to find:

But wild beasts of the desert shall lie there; and their houses shall be full of doleful
*creatures; and owls shall dwell there, and **satyrs** shall dance there.* Isaiah 13:21

Natural History Notes on the Satyr

Artist's impression of Satyrs

Having mentioned the Unicorn we must also mention the Satyr, another fabulous creature, a hairy half man, half goat animal referred to also by the ancient Greeks. Who knows what strange animals lived in bygone days?

There are many strange creatures on the Earth today, some still to be discovered. If Satyrs did dance and howl at night at the destruction of Babylon and Idumea then so be it. 'Doleful creatures' according to Isaiah who referred to them twice.

However, as we are unlikely to know any of the four mentioned above any better then it would be pointless to comment further on them.

Ape

Reference to find:

For the King had at sea a navy of Tharshish with the navy of Hiram:
*once in three years came the navy of Tharshish, bringing gold and silver, ivory and **apes,** and peacocks.*
1 Kings 10:22

Natural History Notes on the Ape

Apes are said to have been part of the cargo of Solomon's ships on their three yearly jaunts and may refer to monkeys. Wall paintings on Egyptian tombs show long-tailed monkeys and we know both monkeys and apes were part of court entertainment. Such is the human intellect! The cephs or apes of Ethiopia are shown as tailless animals.

Sacred Baboon
(Papio hamadryas)

Some monkeys were probably brought to Palestine from India where they are held in considerable reverence. It should be remembered that many riots took place between natives and the British due to the latter having killed monkeys.

However, we know the Ancient Egyptians worshipped, or reverenced, the Baboon and it was ranked highly among their dieties along with bulls and snakes for example. I believe the two likely candidates to be **Silenus veter**, the **Ouanderoo**, sometimes called the lion-tailed Baboon which also has a massive hairy mane, and the **Sacred Baboon, Papio hamadryas**.

The latter derives its scientific name from papio (New L) a baboon and hama (GR) for wood nymph, together with drus (GR) a tree. It inhabits hillsides in Arabia, Ethiopia and Sudan. The former often spelt Wanderoo, could easily have been shipped from India by order of Solomon.

Viper or Adder

The wicked are estranged from the womb:
They go astray as soon as they be born, speaking lies.
Their poison is like the poison of a serpent:
*They are like the deaf **adder** that stoppeth her ear;*
Psalm 58:3,4

Dan shall be a serpent by the way,
*An **adder** in the path,*
That biteth the horse heels,
So that his rider shall fall backward.
Genesis 49:17

Natural History Notes on the Viper or Adder

Silently a viper slithers into purple heather on an Exmoor hillside, away from our footsteps, the zig-zag pattern along its back showing clearly. It had been basking in sunshine on a pathway trod by the feet of many people, dogs and livestock over many centuries. England on a lush summer's day is a far cry from Bible Lands yet as close to our Maker and to Nature, close enough to feel both in our hearts and souls.

When St.Paul was collecting firewood in Malta a Viper fastened itself on his hand, a snake which may have been a **Common Viper (Vipera berus)** though it is no longer seen on this Island.

In Bible Lands there is a **Palestine Viper (Vipera xanthina)** one of the family of true vipers, the viperidae, which is found from the British Isles and Europe, through Africa and across Asia and China.

Adder *(Vipera berus)*

Vipera berus gives birth to live young, whilst the British Grass Snake, for example, lays her eggs to hatch. Strangely the **Levantine viper (V.lebetina lebetina)** found in Cyprus, gives birth to live young yet the very same sub species living in Central Asia Minor, lays eggs! In Britain we tend to use the name Adder rather than Viper. Legend tells us a female adder will swallow her young when danger threatens but actually the young swiftly hide under her belly. Adders are not generally aggressive but they will retaliate if provoked. Male adders in Britain emerge from hibernation in February or March, females slightly later. Courtship usually reaches its peak in April, females becoming pregnant every two years. An adder may live 10 years.

They eat small mammals and will take frogs and toads. A large meal may last a week or so.

In Spring you may see adders swaying and writhing, this 'dance' of the adders being males attempting to win a female. They may vary considerably in colour and markings but a dark zig zag pattern along the back is usual, and a 'v' mark at the back of the head.

Black, melanistic adders are not uncommon. Males are about 24ins (60cms) long, with females often longer. Females are usually duller and browner than males and have less contrast between background colour and markings. They are usually fatter and may reach 30ins (76cms) in length.

An old country saying goes 'some adders venomous and some don't.' Adders are venomous, not poisonous. They can be eaten!

Asp

References to find:

Their throat is an open sepulchre;
With their tongues they have used deceit;
*The poisons of **asps** is under their lips:*
Romans 3.13

*He shall suck the poison of **asps**:*
The viper's tongue shall slay him.
Job 20:16

Natural History Notes on the Asp

The Old Testament tells of the cruel venom of Asps and of course it was Cleopatra's death that is usually remembered when the Asp is mentioned. It seems certain that the **Egyptian Cobra (Naja haje)** is the asp of Bible Lands, a snake which lives in a hole in the ground, not a good place to picnic methinks. The venom of the Egyptian Cobra is very swift acting and works on the nervous system. The snake is found across North Africa and South to Zambia. It is a large snake sometimes reaching 8ft (2.5m) in length.

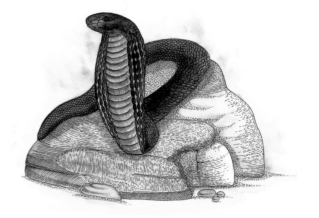

The Egyptian Cobra *(Naja haje)*

Today the only snake correctly referred to as an asp is the **European Asp, (Vipera aspis)**, but at one time a wide array of snakes were called asps. The asp was a symbol of Royalty in dynastic and Roman Egypt and was used as a means of execution for some criminals. An estimated lethal dose for humans is 40-50mg of venom.

Lizard

Reference to find:

*.... and the **lizard** and the snail, and the mole.*
These are unclean to you..." Leviticus 11:30,31

Natural History Notes on the Lizard

Yet another of the so-called 'unclean' animals and thought to refer to the Lacertid family of lizards. A number of lizard species inhabit Bible Lands, including geckoes and the **Large Desert Monitor (Varanus griseus).** The Desert Monitor ranges across the Sahara through Arabia and Iran to Pakistan.

Varanus (New L) a monitor lizard; griseus meaning grey.

Our **Common Lizard (Lacerta vivipara)** has a wider distribution than any other lizard, inhabiting North and Central Europe, the British Isles, and ranging North in Sweden to the Arctic Circle and East to Mongolia. It is a good swimmer and may hunt for prey in water.

Lacerta (L) a lizard; vivipara from vivus (L) alive and pareo (L) I bring forth. Young are born alive in the egg and receive no nourishment from the mother. The young soon break out of the egg membrane and are independent immediately. There is no parental care.

'Our' Common Lizard (*Lacerta vivipara*)

Gecko

Reference to find:

*…. and the **lizard** and the snail, and the mole.*
These are unclean to you…" Leviticus 11:30,31

Natural History Notes on the Gecko

A likely **lizard** of the Bible is the **fan-footed Ptyodactylus Gecko**, a reptile red-brown in colour, with white spots. It exudes a poison from its toes which produces a red rash on humans wherever the feet touch.

There are about 650 species of Geckoes distributed in the warmer regions of the world with only four in Europe. They are mainly small, plump lizards with large heads and eyes. Most are excellent climbers and have claws and sophisticated adhesive pads on the toes.

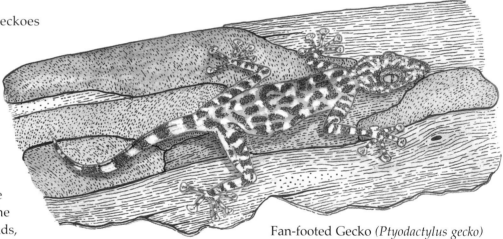

Both the **Moorish Gecko** and the **Turkish Gecko** are found in the Mediterranean region, including islands, and in North Africa.

Fan-footed Gecko (*Ptyodactylus gecko*)

All species of Gecko have immovable eyelids and wipe their eyes clean with the tongue. Many have complicated toes with claws and expanded tips that have specialised scales covered with tiny hairs (scansors) which allow them to climb seemingly smooth surfaces. Most are nocturnal. All lay 1-2 hard shelled eggs. 'Fan-footed' refers to the flared toe tips as found in thick-toed and leaf-toed geckoes.

Tortoise

Reference to find:

*These also shall be unclean unto you among the creeping things that creep upon the earth;
the weasel, and the mouse, and the **tortoise** after his kind,....* Leviticus 11:29,30

Natural History Notes on the Tortoise (Testudo greaca)

The Tortoise (Testudo greaca) is common enough in Bible Lands and probably correctly identified in the Authorised Version of the Bible, even though some translators today prefer 'lizard'. It is a successful species able to survive tough conditions and is disease resistant. It is a favoured food of certain birds of prey.

Testudo, (L) testudinis, a tortoise, of the family Testudinidae, all essentially land tortoises which visit water only for drinking and bathing.

greaca (L) greacus, of Greece. The specific name a bit of a misnomer, certainly misleading as it inhabits large areas of Southern Europe and Northern Africa, East to the Caspian Sea. It is the tortoise sold in pet shops. Restricted to areas with hot summers and found in a variety of moist and dry habitats, cultivated lands, lush meadows, hillsides, light woodlands, and dunes. Prefers dense vegetation areas.

Up to 12 eggs may be laid in loose soil. Hatching time depends on the climate but may take 3 months. Young tortoises are basically similar to adults.

The so-called 'Greek' tortoise is better known as the Spur-thighed. Mediterranean populations have suffered a great deal from over collecting for the pet trade and less commonly for food.

Tortoise *(Testudo greaca)*

Frog

*And if thou refuse to let them go, behold, I will smite all thy borders with **frogs**: and the river shall bring forth **frogs** abundantly, which shall go up and come into thine house, and into thy bedchamber…* Exodus 8:2,3

*Their land brought forth **frogs** in abundance,* Psalm 105:30

Natural History Notes on the Frog

One of the springtime delights of our garden ponds and the ponds and ditches of the countryside. In its own way the first frog spawn of the year heralds the British Spring as much as the first swallow, or call of a cuckoo.

'Our' Common Frog
(Rana temporaria)

We welcome our frogs yet it is one of the Biblical plague creatures which swarmed all over Egypt, mentioned in Exodus. It is also referred to in Revelations.

Modern zoologists agree the genus Rana, the true frogs, is that referred to and they are found almost everywhere. **The Edible Frog (Rana esculenta)** is thought by some to be the frog of the Bible and it is common in Bible Lands today, but evidence is slight. It is a beautiful amphibian and found wherever marshes and water abound. Their night time croaking makes them one of the great nocturnal presences of the Animal Kingdom.

They have established colonies in the South and East of England in the recent past but numbers have declined drastically. Possibly all introduced. They range from France Eastwards through Central Europe to Northern Russia, North to Sweden and South to Italy and the Balkans.

The Common Frog is **Rana temporaria**, one of the Brown Frogs. It is the most widespread and often the commonest frog in Europe. Typical frogs usually assemble in large numbers to breed, males singing in chorus and developing prominent dark nuptial pads on their thumbs. They grasp the female around the body behind the arms. Eggs are laid in large clumps, a female Brown Frog producing up to 2000 or more. Contrary to popular belief frogs spend most of their time on land.

Rana punctata, the **Egyptian Spotted Frog** is the commonest in that country. It has an ash coloured skin dotted with green spots and may well be the 'plague' frog of the Bible.

Whale

*And God created great **whales**, and every living creature that moveth, which the waters brought forth abundantly….* Genesis 1:21

Natural History Notes on the Whale

A difficult one. Translators argue over 'whale' and 'sea monsters', 'great sea serpents' and 'great fish' to the extent no specific whale can be identified. Of course, the whales are not fish anyway so that rules them out of the Jonah story. If we are to accept and believe the word of the Bible then we ought not to pick and choose what suits us. We should either take it on board or not otherwise we are merely 'writing' the Bible ourselves.

'the Lord had prepared a great fish to swallow up Jonah', (Jonah 1:17). That's it really. Either He did or He didn't, but either way it wasn't a whale.

Artist's impression of a Whale

Genesis refers to whales in the Creation, and they are mentioned in Ezekiel and Job. Modern translators have wavered and the whale has virtually declined from modern translations. Sad that.

While it would be fruitless to specify any Whale of Bible waters in terms of the Bible itself, readers will be interested to know that the Humpback Whale and other mysticete (baleen) whales spend summers in Polar regions where they put on 50-70 per cent of their body weight in blubber, gorging on krill. At the beginning of the winter the Humpback migrates some 7000km to sub-tropical waters where there may not be much food, to give birth, suckle their young and mate. It would seem warm waters are the attraction, possibly better for the young ones. Actual travel presents few problems, for example, a Fin Whale tagged in Icelandic Waters was found 1,700kms away 10 days later.

Horse

References to find:

And a chariot came up and went out of Egypt for six hundred shekels of silver, and an **horse** *for an hundred and fifty:* 1 Kings 10:29

And Miriam answered them,
Sing ye to the Lord, for he hath triumphed gloriously;
The **horse** *and his rider hath he thrown into the sea.* Exodux 15:21

Natural History Notes on the Horse

A truly noble animal and Biblically the horse is a symbol of strength and speed and rightly so. It is used mainly as a metaphor.

The Horse, along with Tapirs and Rhinoceroses are of the group Perissodactyla and along with pigs, cattle, antelopes and their kin are ungulates. Ungulate means hoofed, from the Latin unguis, a claw or hoof.

Perissodactyla means 'odd-toed', the members of this group having one or three toes. Rhinoceroses have three toes on each foot. Tapirs are an exception in having three toes on the hind feet, four on the front feet.

Horse (*Equus caballus)*

In all cases the central axis of the foot passes through the third digit, which takes most of its weight and is large and symmetrical. In the case of horses, asses and zebras it is the only digit remaining and thus takes all the weight. The others disappeared during an evolutionary process of over 18 million years. So, they walk and run on their middle fingers so to speak.

The order is divided into two sub-orders, Hippomorpha, the 'horse-kind', and Ceratomorpha, the 'horned-kind'. The antelope group having an even number of toes or hooves are named Artiodactyla, meaning 'even-toed'.

Horse, Equus caballus; caballus (L) a pack-horse, a nag; the domestic horse.

Adult male, a stallion; female, a mare; young horse a foal.

Ass

References to find:

*…. then sent Jesus two disciples, saying unto them, Go into the village over against you,
and straight-way ye shall find an **ass** tied, and a colt with her:* Matthew 21:2

*And so shall be the plague of the horse, of the mule, of the camel, and of the **ass**,
and of all the beasts that shall be in these tents, as this plague.* Zechariah 14:15

Natural History Notes on the Ass

African Wild Ass
(Equus asinus)

One feels sorry for the Ass as a beast of burden as it always seems so overloaded, a hard working, faithful animal. People drank, and still drink, asses milk but do not eat its flesh. Animals with undivided hooves, that chewed the cud were forbidden meat.

Christ came as a messenger of peace riding on an Ass, not as a conqueror so the animal has a pleasant history on those terms.

The **Somali Wild Ass** is **Equus asinus**, a delightful animal, according to some books, but the scientific name given to the Domestic Ass by Linnaeus in 1758.

Equus (L) a horse; asinus (L) an ass.

The **African Wild Ass, E.africanus** is generally accepted as the ancestor of the Domestic Donkey, but is becoming very rare.

Note: A mule is the offspring of a male Ass mating with a mare, the female horse. It would be sterile and could not breed.

The Mule is mentioned over 20 times in the Old Testament and King Solomon rode one when proclaimed King. It was greatly valued as a pack animal with more endurance and sure footedness than horses.

Swine

References to find:

*As a jewel of gold in a **swine's** snout,*
So is a fair woman which is without discretion. Proverbs 11:22

*… and he sent him into his fields to feed **swine**.*
*And he would fain have filled his belly with the husks that the **swine** did eat: and no man gave unto him.* Luke 15:15,16

Natural History Notes on Swine

Not popular in terms of its meat in Bible Lands with some saying the flesh of pigs can harbour parasites which may transfer to humans if not properly cooked. But even the living animal caused revulsion in many, with scholars suggesting the pig was taboo amongst ancient Egyptians as it turned up the earth with its snout and thus first taught man to plough. Why was that thought so wrong one wonders? And the prodigal son was employed to feed swine (Luke 15) and that must have been for food methinks.

To see a long snout typical of the Wild Boar, in a modern British Pig see the Tamworth whose orange-red colouring is from an imported West Indian pig.

The Tamworth Pig

Boar

Reference to find:

*The **boar** out of the wood doth waste it,*
And the wild beast of the field doth devour it. Psalm 80:13

Natural History Notes on the Wild Boar (Sus scrofa)

The Wild Boar (Sus scrofa) is mentioned only once as such and that laid waste a vineyard. It was common in Bible Lands just a century ago and found all along the banks of the River Jordan.

This is the ancestor of the domestic pig and is a true forest dweller. It will eat virtually anything edible from vegetation and animals, tree roots to small mammals.

It has been extinct in Britain since the early 17th century but introductions are currently being attempted, with problematical releases occurring from animal rights people who set them free to roam the countryside.

The Wild Boar must be the Biblical "beast of the reeds" for it loves woods and reed beds, wallowing in mud, and evidently a destroyer of vineyards, without doubt an extremely powerful animal and dangerous adversary when persecuted.

Sus scrofa then, Sus (L) a pig, scrofa (L) a breeding sow, the boar from which domestic pigs have been derived. It has a widespread distribution including Europe, North Africa, Asia, Sumatra, Java, Formosa and Japan.

Wild Boar *(Sus scrofa)*

Sheep

References to find:

*And Abel was a keeper of **sheep**, but Cain was a tiller of the ground.* Genesis 4:2

*And David said unto Saul, Thy servant kept his father's **sheep**, and there came a lion, and a bear,*
and took a lamb out of the flock: and I went out after him, and smote him, and delivered it out of his mouth: 1 Samuel 17:34,35

Natural History Notes on Sheep

An important animal in Bible Lands with over 500 references including those to Ewe and Ram.

They were a measure of prosperity and a form of currency to some, with huge flocks owned by some such as Abraham, Isaac and Jacob.

As well as important in real terms, sheep play a huge part metaphorically in the Bible, Christ Himself being both the 'Lamb of God' and the 'Good Shepherd'.

The actual ancestry of the **Domestic Sheep (Ovis aries)** is uncertain and there are over 400 different breeds. It was first domesticated thousands of years ago. Ovis (L) a Sheep; aries (L) a Ram.

The Mouflon (O.musimon) is Sardinian and considered to be one of the ancestors of the domestic sheep.

Sheep are of the Order Artiodactyla, even-toed ungulates, an Order which includes pigs, cows, goats, deer, antelopes and others.

The Domestic Sheep (*Ovis aries*)

The Soay or Wild Sheep was probably introduced to the island of Soay in the St.Kilda group over 1000 years ago by the Vikings. It is the most primitive of domestic breeds in Britain and Europe, resembling sheep of Neolithic times. In the 1930s they were introduced to the neighbouring island of Hirta and more recently to various sites around Britain where some are used as a grassland conservation 'tool' for grazing regimes.

Adult male, ram; female, ewe and young are lambs.

The Mouflon (*Ovis musimon*)
Ancestor of the domestic sheep.

Camel

References to find:

*And Rebekah lifted up her eyes, and when she saw Isaac, she lighted off the **camel**.* Genesis 24:64

*And again I say unto you, It is easier for a **camel** to go through the eye of a needle,*
than for a rich man to enter into the kingdom of God. Matthew 19:24

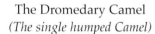

The Dromedary Camel
(The single humped Camel)

Natural History Notes on the Camel

One of the earliest animals referred to in the Bible, the well known 'ship of the desert'. The Dromedary has a single hump, the Bactrian Camel, two. Its home is the desert, the perfect animal creation for such a harsh habitat, sure footed, able to go for long periods without food and water and eating but little when coarse, prickly shrubs are available though it eats these with ease. A tireless, wonderful animal, sadly a slave to humans.

Its stomach has a number of sacs capable of retaining large amounts of water for a long time.

Cattle

Highland Cattle
(heads)
An example of
Longhorn Cattle

Reference to find:

…Give us bread: for why should we die in thy presence? for the money faileth.
*And Joseph said, Give your **cattle**; and I will give you for your **cattle**, if money fail.* Genesis 47:15,16

*Your wives, your little ones, and your **cattle**, shall remain in the land which Moses gave you on this side Jordan;* Joshua 1:14

Natural History Notes on Cattle

450 references to Cattle, important possessions and close to being wild cattle, horned, shaggy coated, left to feed and roam and sometimes brought in in winter and fed barley.

In Britain Long Horn Cattle go back centuries and from the very earliest records of British Agriculture there has been a race set apart from most other breeds by the great length of their horns. In the original types the horns projected nearly horizontally on either side of the head. However, as cattle were improved, horns changed direction, mostly in the shape known as wheel horns.

A Staffordshire farmer writing in 1876 spoke of Longhorn Cattle being in his family for 280 years, and one Sir Thomas Gresley of Burton-Upon-Trent kept a diary of such cattle in the early 1700s.

Deer

References to find:

And Solomon's provision for one day was thirty measures of fine flour,
and three score measures of meal, ten fat oxen, and twenty oxen out of the pastures,
*and an hundred sheep, beside **harts**, and **roebucks**, and **fallow deer**, and fatted fowl.* 1 Kings 4:22,23

And there were three sons of Zeruiah there, Joab, and Abishai, and Asahel:
*and Asahel was as light of foot as a **wild roe**.* 2 Samuel 2:18

Natural History Notes on Deer

Translation is a funny thing. It seems that 'Roe and Roebuck', in the Bible around 17 times, should probably have been 'gazelle' all along. However, hart, hind and fallow deer can be left as any or all Red Deer, Fallow Deer and the Roe, as each lived in Bible Lands once upon a time.

Well, to us the hart is a male red deer, or stag, and hind is the female red deer. Roe deer males are bucks, females, does, and the young are fawns as opposed to young red deer who are calves. Fallow deer are named the same as the roe.

Of these species the **Roe Deer (Capreolus capreolus)** is the only one still found in Bible Lands and then only as a rarity these days. Evidently the Roe was the emblem of the Naphthali tribe whose land stretched along the hill country overlooking the Hula Valley in the North.

The Roe Deer (*Capreolus capreolus*)   The Red Deer (*Cervus elaphus*)   The Fallow Deer (*Dama dama*)

In Britain the **Red Deer (Cervus elaphus)** and the Roe, are common in the countryside but the **Fallow Deer (Dama dama)** is more of a park and estate animal.

The Fallow Deer is still found in most countries, however, and there have been introductions from Europe. Descendants of original herds still living wild in Cannock Chase, Epping Forest and The New Forest. Present distribution largely due to escapes.

The Roe Deer has become more widespread and common partly due to afforestation and is indigenous in Britain and in the Palaearctic Region, but not in Ireland. Many introductions have been made, some from Germany, and the Roe is still increasing its range and found in every county in Scotland. Melanism is not uncommon in this species with dark coloured winter coats being notable.

The Red Deer is very much a Scottish and Exmoor animal but is found in several British counties. Its full distribution is throughout the Palaearctic Region from Ireland and the Scottish Hebrides to Manchuria and from just South of the Arctic Circle in Norway to the Himalayas and North Africa. It has been introduced in USA, Argentina, Australia and New Zealand.

Wild Goat

References to find:

*The high hills are a refuge for the **wild goats**;*
And the rocks for the conies. Psalm 104:18

*Knowest thou the time when the **wild goats** of the rock bring forth?* Job 39:1

Natural History Notes on the Wild Goat

The Wild Goat referred to in the Bible is likely to have been the **Nubian Ibex (Capra nubiana)** and not the ancestor of the **Domestic Goat (Capra hircus).** It is fairly certain the true wild goat was extinct long before Old Testament days though it was once found in Bible Lands.

The Ibex looks very much like a goat and is closely related. The Ibex has long been considered as a sort of walking medicine chest, every part of its body good for curing some ailment or simply to strengthen us in various ways. Thus they were extensively hunted and the Ibex is now a protected species in Bible Lands in the area of En Gedi where David sought refuge from Saul.

The wild goat found in Britain today is more properly a feral goat and has descended, with some cross breeding, with other races, from the **Persian pasang or Grecian Ibex (Capra hircus aegagrus).** The pasang's range is extensive and it is found on a number of islands in the Aegean Sea, East to the Caucasus, Asia Minor and Iran (Persia).

Wild goat *(Capra aegagrus)*

Nubian Ibex
(Capra nubiana)

According to some zoologists there is no evidence to show that the goat was ever indigenous to Britain and it is thought to have been introduced here during the Neolithic period when the British Isles were still joined to the landmass. Along with the sheep and Ox it was one of the earliest domesticated animals to be imported.

Wild Goat. Capra aegagrus.
 Capra (L) a she goat; aigos, a goat; agrios (GR) living in the fields, wild. Thought to be the ancestor of the domestic goat. Also known as the Bezoar Goat.

Chameleon

Reference to find:

*....and the ferret, and the **chameleon**, and the lizard and the snail, and the mole.*
(Shall be unclean unto you) Leviticus 11:30

The Chameleon
(Chamaeleo chameleon)

Natural History Notes on the Chameleon

Mentioned once only and more translation problems but there are Chameleons in the Bible Lands today and about 80 species in the world. The **Common Chameleon** is **Chamaeleo chameleon.** Most of us have been taught that chameleons change colour to camouflage themselves to match their surroundings but it seems the pigmentation alterations are responses to emotions, temperature and light intensity. Some turn black when very angry.

Chamois

Reference to find:

These are the beasts which ye shall eat: the ox, the sheep, and the goat, the hart, and the roebuck,
*and the fallow deer, and the wild goat and the pygarg, and the wild ox, and the **chamois**.* Deuteronomy 14:4,5

Natural History Notes on the Chamois

The Chamois, **Rupicapra rupicapra** has not been recorded wild in Bible Lands and is found in the Alps and the Pyrenees. The Chamois of Deuteronomy 14.5.has been renamed 'mountain sheep'.

Mountain Sheep
Cyprus Sheep
(Ovis ammon ophion)

Ferret

References to find:

*....and the **ferret**, and the chameleon, and the lizard and the snail, and the mole. (Shall be unclean unto you)*
Leviticus 11:30

Natural History Note on the Ferret

More translation problems, Bible scholars now choosing Hedgehog, Shrew Mouse and Gecko for 'ferret'....

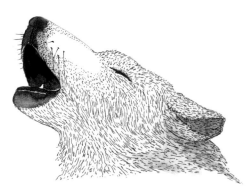

'Our' Hedgehog
(*Erinaceus europaeus*)

Wolf

References to find:

*Wherefore a lion out of the forest shall slay them, and a **wolf** of the evenings shall spoil them, a leopard shall watch over their cities:*
Jeremiah 5:6

*But he that is an hireling, and not the shepherd, whose own the sheep are not, seeth the **wolf** coming, and leaveth the sheep, and fleeth:*
John 10:12

Natural History Notes on the Wolf

Wolves were not popular in the Bible, none of the 13 references being complimentary. The wolf of Bible Lands is **Canis lupus lupus,** the **Grey Wolf,** a smallish species still to be found in the wild. It inhabits the wilder areas of Northern Europe, North America and Canada and Asia.

Canis (L) a dog; lupus (L) a wolf.

Extinct in England since the reign of Henry VIII, in Scotland since 1743 and Ireland in the 1760s. The last wolf on the mainland of Great Britain was killed in Morayshire in 1743.

The Grey Wolf Howling
(*Canis lupus lupus*)

Man's hatred for the wolf in agricultural areas of Europe harks back to generations of mis-information and false tales. Even accurate estimates of kills by wolves should not breed the animosity it does. The infamous Varmland situation between Stockholm and Oslo is a case in point. Fury at wolves taking about 200 sheep in a year when it is known 95,000 die of natural causes before coming to market! And for wolves to be killing too many elk where hunters shoot 125,000 a year!

A genetic problem occurs it seems, in that some she-wolves mate with shepherd dogs. Though no doubt this has been occurring through history the wild wolf is so scarce now it faces extinction due to genetic dilution. One supposes they are the same species effectively and referring to them as a distinctive species could be said to be more a matter of convenience, linked to over 10,000 years of domestication as far as 'the shepherd dog' is concerned.

A more tolerant attitude and introduction of many more deer to augment the prey/food situation is much needed.

The Grey Wolf
(*Canis lupus lupus*)

Jackal

Reference to find:

Therefore I will wail and howl, I will go stripped and naked: I will make a wailing like the dragons, and mourning as the owls.
Micah 1:8

And in comparison, here is the same quotation from the NIV (New International Version of the Bible)

I will moan and cry because of this evil. I will go around bare foot and without clothes.
*I will cry loudly like the **wild dogs**. I will cry like the ostriches* Micah 1:8 (NIV)

Natural History Notes on the Jackal

The Jackal is linked with desolation in the Bible and some species look rather like foxes. Jackal's however, hunt in packs and are also carrion eaters. They are the most numerous beast of prey in Bible Lands. The **Common or Golden Jackal, Canis aureus** inhabits South

Eastern Europe, Central and Northern Africa, the Middle East and much of Southern Asia including Thailand, but not Malaysia.

Canis (L) a dog and aureus (L) golden.

Jackals are generally successful and prolific, breeding once a year and bearing 3-8 young. They are sexually mature at around 12 months and have a gestation period of two months or so.

The Golden Jackal
(*Canis aureus*)

Hyena

Reference to find:

And the wild beasts of the islands shall cry in their desolate houses, and dragons in their pleasant places: and her time is near to come, and her days shall not be prolonged. Isaiah 13:22

And in comparison, here is the same quotation from the NIV (New International Version of the Bible)

Wolves will howl within the strong walls. **Wild Dogs** *will bark in the beautiful buildings. The end of Babylon is near. Its time is almost over.* Isaiah 13:22 (NIV)

Natural History Notes on the Hyena

Very common in Bible Lands and found in a variety of habitats. The male **Striped Hyena (Hyaena hyaena)** may weigh up to 80lbs. They are now protected by law.

Hyenas feed at night on small animals and carrion and always leave off feeding at daybreak. They have a well established 'pecking order', pregnant females being allowed priority at carrion situations.

The Striped Hyena has 6 vertical stripes on the flanks. It inhabits Africa, the Near East and India.

Hyena, from Lus (GR) a hog, on account of the bristly mane, which all hyenas have though it normally lies flat.

Hyena (*Hyaena hyaena*)

Coney

References to find:

The high hills are a refuge for the wild goats;
*And the rocks for the **conies**.* Psalm 104:18

Natural History Notes on the Coney

The **Coney** is referred to in Leviticus, Deuteronomy, Psalm 104 and in Proverbs, the latter stating 'the conies are but a feeble folk, yet they make their houses among the rocks'. Whilst it is true that at the time of the Authorised or King James 1st Version of the Bible the word 'cony' meant **rabbit**, from the Latin Cuniculus it seems translators agree the animal referred to is the **Rock or Syrian Hyrax** which is not related to rabbits.

This is **Procavia capensis syriacus** which ranges through Syria and Siani and South to Saudi Arabia. A substance called hyraceum secreted by the hyrax was used medicinally against epilepsy and convulsions. It is a distant relative of the rhinoceros and the elephant.

Rock Hyrax
(Procavia capensis syriacus)

And in comparison, 'our' Rabbit
(Oryctolagus cuniculus)

Fox

Reference to find:

*Now Tobiah the Ammonite was by him, and he said, Even that which they build, if a **fox** go up, he shall even break down their stone wall.*

Nehemiah 4:3

*And he said unto them, Go ye, and tell that **fox**, Behold, I cast out devils,*
and I do cures to day and to morrow, and the third day I shall be perfected. Luke 13:32

Natural History Notes on the Fox

The Fox of the Bible is difficult to pin down. A few references are now said more likely to refer to the Jackal, but not all. The Red Fox we know in Britain and Europe may be the Biblical Fox but a sub-species **Vulpes vulpes niloticus** lays some claim and there is the little **Fennec Fox (Fennecus zerda)** of Bible lands.

Fenek is an Arabic word for a small fox. It inhabits North Africa.

The European Red Fox inhabits Britain and Europe, North America, North Africa, Asia and India.

The Fennec Fox (*Fennecus zerda*)

Bible references suggest foxes take grapes. They certainly eat blackberries, the fruit of the bramble, in the British Isles for I have seen them do so on several occasions. They hunt small mammals, some birds, eat fungi and carrion.

The European Red Fox
(*Vulpes vulpes*)

It is a member of the Order Carnivora and the Canidae, or dog family of which it is the only wild representative in Britain. It is found in most habitats and nowadays lives and breeds in our towns and cities.

The fox normally lives in a den called an earth, breeding dens needing to be dry and close to an available food supply. Mating is usually December into February and vixens are on heat for only about 3 days. The gestation period is 51-63 days and towards the end of this time the vixen remains below ground most of the time, the dog fox bringing her food. Cubs are usually born between March and May, usually 3-5 being born. Most are weaned by 30-40 days. The vixen teaches the cubs to hunt, occasionally aided by the dog fox.

Foxes feed mainly on rats, voles, mice, rabbits, and some insects and earthworms. Sheep and deer eaten are usually carrion. A few survive to 4 years with rare examples living to 6 years.

Greyhound

Reference to find:

*A **greyhound**; an he goat also;*
And a king, against whom there is no rising up. Proverbs 30:31

Natural History Notes on the Greyhound

Referred to in Proverbs but nowadays cast aside as an unlikely translation. Indeed readers may be amused at various translations from the Hebrew, including Wild Ass, Warhorse, and even a wrestler! All have 'girded loins' in one way or another. Greyhounds were and are used for hunting in Bible Lands.

The Greyhound (*Canis familiaris leineri*)

Dog

References to find:

So he brought down the people unto the water: and the Lord said unto Giddeon,
Everyone that lappeth of the water with his tongue,
*as a **dog** lappeth, him shalt thou set by himself;*
likewise every one that boweth down upon his knees to drink. Judges 7:5

*For to him that is joined to all the living there is hope: for a living **dog** is better than a dead lion.* Ecclesiastes 9:4

Natural History Notes of the Dog

Dogs were useful in Biblical times as scavengers and therefore cleaners of rotting flesh at rubbish heaps, and as guardians of livestock flocks. The Pariah Dog of Bible Lands is a sub-species of Canis familiaris and is reckoned to have bred with Jackals and wolves. A good cross breed methinks. They live and hunt in packs but usually return to their respective lairs by day.

Jesus wasn't too keen when a Canaanite woman tossed bread scraps to the dogs but He was told that the dogs were allowed to eat the scraps that fell from the Master's table. Quite right too.

So important today are dogs, shepherding sheep, leading the blind, listening for the deaf, and as companions for so many of us across the world.

A Greyhound'ís Head
(*Canis familiaris leineri*)

If I have to end this animal section of Endymion's book with a thought it is that when humans humble up a bit and respect animals for who and what they are, God's creatures if you like, then the world will be a better place. I don't care what those in the Bible might have said in derogatory fashion, about animals over the years, they are part of God's Creation, not to be abominated. There tis......

Leopard

*Can the Ethiopian change his skin, or the **leopard** his spots?* Jeremiah 13.23

*The wolf also shall dwell with the lamb, and the **leopard** shall lie down with the kid;* Isaiah 11:6

Natural History Notes on the Leopard

The Leopard, Panthera pardus is mentioned in the Old and New Testaments and, in the 'Song of Solomon' , referred to along with lions. Whether the leopard will lie down with the kid as prophesised we will have to wait and see. It does now but usually when eating it.

What is fascinating in Britain and Europe is that in recent years we have leopard, puma and a few smaller species of 'strange' cats in the countryside from escapes and releases from captive situations. This includes both Ireland and France according to information sent to me.

Black big-cats, which in my view are black leopards or panthers, and pumas, have both bred in the wild and seen with cubs and sub adults. Thus we have an interesting feral big-cat situation in Britain thanks to irresponsible owners.

The genus Panthera includes all the big-cats, lion, tiger and leopard.

It is thought the Biblical leopard is referring to any of three cats, the leopard proper, (Panthera pardus) the once (Uncia uncia) and the Cheetah or Hunting Leopard (Acinonyx jubatus) all of which are found in Biblical Lands.

Leopard (*Panthera pardus*)

Lion

References to find:

And of Gad he said,
Blessed be he that enlargeth Gad:
*He dwelleth as a **lion**,*
And teareth the arm with the crown of the head.
Deuteronomy 33:20

And of Dan he said,
*Dan is a **lion's** whelp:*
He shall leap from Bashan.
Deuteronomy 33:22

*And after a time he returned to take her, and he turned aside to see the carcase of the **lion**:*
*and, behold, there was a swarm of bees and honey in the carcase of the **lion**.* Judges 14:8

Natural History Notes on the Lion

156 references to the **lion (Panthera leo),** a big-cat more legendary in Bible times than even today, and used mainly in metaphorical manner. It was a lion that lamed Noah for forgetting to feed it in the Ark.

Lions were well known in Bible Lands but are said to have been extinct in the wild for over a century. They were common in Palestine so it is not surprising that the Bible contains so many references to them. The lion has a reputation for kindness and magnanimity which has come down through the ages.

The earliest true lions appeared in Europe 600,000 years ago and these early cave lions are thought to be the largest cats that ever lived, some 25 percent larger than today's largest lions.

Lion (*Panthera leo*)

Badger

References to find:

*I clothed thee also with broidered work, and shod thee with **badgers' skin**,*
and I girded thee about with fine linen, and I covered thee with silk. Ezekiel 16:10

*...and they shall put it and all the vessels thereof within a covering of **badgers' skins,** and shall put it upon a bar.* Numbers 4:10

Natural History Notes on the Badger

Badger (*Meles meles*)

Biblical references to the badger invariably relate to the pelts used as offerings and not to live badgers. Quite luxurious must have been the tents so covered with ram's skins and badger's skins. It seems even the Ark of the Covenant may have been so covered.

Both the **Honey Badger (Mellivora capensis)** and our own **European Badger (Meles meles)** have been recorded in Bible Lands. In the times of the Authorised version of the Bible badgers were thought to have magical powers.

An old belief that badgers have shorter legs on the left side than on the right entered British folklore many years ago. It was thought Old Brock could move more easily across horizontal hillsides, and in wheel ruts but no-one explained the difficulty of return journeys.

Mellivora, mellis (L) honey; voro (L) I devour. Another name for the Honey Badger is Ratel, possibly from the Dutch raat, a honeycomb.

Meles, (L) a badger.

Our badger is well known and currently common in the British Isles. Its main food is earthworms, supplemented by beetles, some cereals and autumn fruits, small mammals to the size of young rabbits, and the contents of wasp and bee nests. May live for up to 15 years.

The badger lives communally in burrow systems called setts, usually constructed in woodland. The sett includes sleeping chambers where bedding, usually straw, leaves, bracken and some green plants, is held twixt forepaws and chin to be dragged back into the sett.

Cubs are born from mid January to mid March, usually 2-3 to a litter. Some grow up and remain with the family group, others may disperse to seek new territories. Badgers do not hibernate but become less active from December to February and live mainly off fat laid down under their skin in autumn. Mating may be anytime between February and October.

Adult male, a boar; female a sow; young are cubs.

Bear

Reference to find:

*And behold another beast, a second, like to a **bear**, and it raised up itself on one side, and it had three ribs in the mouth of it between the teeth of it:* Daniel 7:5

Natural History Notes on the Bear

Possibly the **Brown Bear (Ursus arctos)** which is found over a large part of the northern hemisphere, the Mediterranean Brown Bear considerably smaller than its North American counterpart. There is also a **Syrian Bear, U.arctos syriacus**. The bear is mentioned 13 times in the Old Testament and once in the New.

The Brown Bear inhabits North America from Alaska south to northern Mexico, central Europe in afforested mountain country and most of Eurasia.

Bear (*Ursus arctos*)

73

Bat

*In that day a man shall cast his idols of silver, and his idols of gold, which they made each one for himself to worship, to the moles and to the **bats**;* Isaiah 2:20

Serotine Bat
(Eptesicus serotinus)

Natural History Notes on the Bat

In Bible Lands there are over 20 species of Bat, mostly small and insectivorous: Our own **Pipistrelle (Pipistrellus pipistrellus)** has a wide range and is found in Britain, and Ireland, East to Japan, Kashmir and Taiwan.

Other 'British' Bats found in Bible Lands include the **Noctule**, **Leisler's Bat** and the **Serotine Bat**.

Pipistrelle Bat's Head
(Pipistrellus pipistrellus)

Weasel

Reference to find:

*These also shall be unclean unto you among the creeping things that creep upon the earth; the **weasel**, and the mouse....* Leviticus 11:29

Natural History Notes on the Weasel

The weasel is referred to only once in the Bible and is most likely Mustela nivalis, our own weasel whose range is across Northern and Central Europe, North Africa and Asia, as well as North America.

The Weasel is about 8ins (20cms) head and body, with a 2ins (5cms) tail and is the smallest British Carnivore. It is a fierce hunter by day and night and often moves in undulating bounds of 12ins (30cms) or more at considerable speed.

Weasel *(Mustela nivalis)*

Weasels are territorial to some extent, size of territory depending on food availability, females using much smaller territories than males. Much over lapping occurs.

Young are born in April or May with second litters in July or August in good summers. Youngsters hunt with their mother as a pack until about 3 months old. Young weasels born early in the year may be capable of breeding in their first summer. Voles and mice are the main food, with rats and rabbits taken, plus some birds and nestlings if the chance occurs. Prey is usually killed with a bite to the back of the neck. A weasel eats about 1oz (28g) of food daily, about 25 per cent of its body weight.

Greater Mole Rat
(*Spalax microphthalmus ehrenbergi*)

Mole

Reference to find:

….and the ferret, and the chameleon, and the lizard and the snail, and the **mole***.* (Shall be unclean unto you) Leviticus 11:30

Natural History Notes on the Mole

The mole as we know it is not found in Bible Lands and the mole of the Bible is said to be the **Palestine Mole Rat, Spalax ehrenbergi,** a similar animal which lives beneath the ground. It has extensive burrows with sleeping chambers, storage areas and connecting passages and lives on roots of grass, trees and shrubs. They range north to Palestine and to East Russia.

Spalax (GR) a mole; ehrenbergi from Dr C. Ehrenberg who worked in North Africa in the 1820s where these animals live. It is also known as the Palestine Mole Rat to differentiate between it and the **African Mole Rat, Tachyorctes splendens.**

And in comparison...
'our' Mole (*Talpa europaea*)

Takhus (GR) fast, swift; oruktes (GR) one who digs; splendeo (L) I shine, some having a black shiny coat.

Mouse

They that sanctify themselves, and purify themselves in the gardens behind one tree in the midst,
eating swine's flesh, and the abomination, and the **mouse***, shall be consumed together saith the Lord.*

Isaiah 66:17

Natural History Notes on the Mouse

Mice feature only in the Old Testament with references being uncomplimentary. Field mice certainly exist in Bible Lands with **Apodemus sylvaticus** being common and occasionally having population explosions.

This is also our own wood mouse or long-tailed field mouse which lives as happily in open country as in woods, as well as around human habitation, with a liking for gardens and sheds. Breeding begins in March and a female may have four litters in a year, each of 3-5 young usually. Their life span is only about two years in the wild. Young are born in a nest chamber in the burrows system. The main food is seeds, with shoots, buds and small snails also taken. They often lay up caches of autumn fruits and berries for winter, sometimes using the old nests of birds as larders.

Woodmouse
(Apodemus sylvaticus)

Many are taken by predators such as foxes, stoats, weasels, owls and birds of prey.

Mainly nocturnal they dig their own burrows where they store food and spend much of the day.

Apodemus (GR) away from home; in the field; sylvaticus, from silva, a wood, silvaticus, of woods or trees. Inhabits Britain and Europe, North Africa and parts of Asia.

Hare

Reference to find:

Nevertheless these ye shall not eat of them that chew the cud, or of them that divide the cloven hoof;
*as the camel and the **hare**, and the coney:* Deuteronomy 14:7

Natural History Notes on the Hare

The Hare, that most magical of animals is featured in the Bible and is a subspecies of the **European** or **Brown Hare, Lepus capensis,** somewhat smaller and paler than our own. It still lives in the grassy lowlands of Bible Lands, having 1-4 leverets at a time and living in forms, the grassy depressions in the open just as ours does. There is also the **Desert Hare, Lepus europeus syriacus.**

Actually the Brown Hare of the British Isles and Europe, is now considered to belong to the Afro-Mediterranean species complex of **L.capensis** and thus by law of priority L.capensis named by Linneaus in 1758 has precedence over L.europaeus named so by Pallas in 1778. This means it is now a subspecies **Lepus capensis europaeus**, which ranges through Europe, Africa and Western Asia.

The **Blue or Scottish Hare, Lepus timidus scoticus** is a subspecies of the **Alpine Hare L.timidus timidus**, and lives in the Scottish highlands.

The Alpine Hare lives in the Alps of Europe and the Scandinavian mountains and Eastwards as far as Japan.

Brown Hare *(Lepus capensis europaeus)*

Ant

References to find:

*Go to the **ant**, thou sluggard;*
Consider her ways, and be wise:
Proverbs 6:6

*The **ants** are a people not strong,*
Yet they prepare their meat in the summer;
Proverbs 30:25

Natural History Notes on the Ant

We move a flagstone in the garden path to redesign some flower beds and immediately scores of ants begin to hustle and bustle about, seeking to find if we have done any damage to their longstanding home. They are industrious insects always looking to the needs and safety of their community.

In Palestine ants are abundant with a variety of species existing, some bringing out their seed stores if they get wet and drying them in the sunshine.

'Our' Black garden Ant
(Lasius niger)

Mentioned briefly but nicely as an example of how we should be industrious, not lazy. It is good to know ancient observers were correct in stating the ant 'provideth her meat in the summer and gathereth her food in the harvest' for some species do. Both the **Black Ant** and the **Brown Ant (Atta barbara** and **Atta structor)** store grain for the winter as but part of their fascinating lifestyles.

About 50 species of ant live in Britain and not all are native species. Some, including the **Argentine ant (Iridomyrmex humilis)** and the **Pharoah's ant (Monomorium pharaonis)** were introduced from the tropics, the former as long ago as 1900. Thus these species only survive in heated buildings, but who knows, with Climate Change, what might happen.

The workers are the ants we normally see. Different species may be carnivorous or vegetarian, some are both, but all will 'milk' aphids and scale insects of the sweet secretion we call honeydew, whenever an opportunity arises. Many species have powerful jaws and a sting. Only females carry a sting as it is a modified egg laying organ. Males and queen ants have wings. These are used just the once during courtship flight. After this nuptial, airborne meeting the males die and the queen rubs or pulls off her wings.

We see this phenomenon annually, usually in August, when swarms take place over a whole area, often during hot, thundery weather. Our attention is often drawn to it by flocks of screaming, wheeling gulls, swallows, swifts and martins all exploiting the situation for food.

The species will be the **Black Garden Ant (Lasius niger)** a common ant of our gardens, grasslands, heaths and woodlands. It is the only native British ant to regularly enter houses but it does not live there. The workers are foragers and are seeking sweet foods. When workers meet they may pass their antennae over one another to aid recognition, each colony having a different and distinctive scent.

Pygarg

Reference to find:

*These are the beasts which ye shall eat: the ox, the sheep, and the goat, the hart, and the roebuck, and the fallow deer, and the wild goat, and the **pygarg**,....* Deuteronomy 14:4,5

Natural History Notes on the Pygarg

Pygargs can be eaten! So says the Bible. It appears a pygarg is a **North African antelope (Addax nasomaculatus)** well adapted for desert life and able to manage on dry vegetation and little water for long periods. Much hunted and also raised in captivity it is now almost extinct in the wild. A population is protected in Hai-Bar Nature Reserve to save it from extinction. (See end of book.)

Addax (L) a wild animal with crooked horns; nasus (L) the nose and macual (L) a spot or mark; atus (L) suffix meaning provided with. The animal has brown patches on its nose and spirally twisted horns. Still found in the Sahara Desert region.

Scorpion

References to find:

*And to them it was given that they should not kill them, but that they should be tormented five months: and their torment was as the torment of the **scorpion**, when he striketh a man.* Revelations 9:5

*Or if he shall ask an egg, will he offer him a **scorpion**?* Luke 11:12

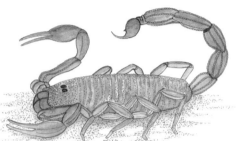

An example of a Scorpion

Natural History Notes on the Scorpion

No argument about scorpions being mis-translated in the Bible. No mistaking these creatures.

Drive them away with violet or parsnip seeds, or have a hare as a companion as the hare is not bothered by them.

They are the Order of Scorpionida, of the Arachnid Class, terrestrial animals with a body divided in two parts. Scorpions are rather long, their abdomen usually having 12 segments, the last 6 forming the tail which ends in the sting. Species vary from half an inch (1¼ cms) to 8ins (20cms) in length and are found in a variety of colours from red, brown, yellow, pale grey and slate grey, the latter being almost black.

Palmerworm

Reference to find:

*I have smitten you with blasting and mildew: when your gardens and your vineyards and your fig trees and your olive trees increased, the **palmerworm** devoured them:* Amos 4:9

Natural History Notes on the Palmerworm

If we are asked about plagues in the Bible most of us would call to mind Locust I reckon. Well the palmerworm is a stage in the life of the locust, no doubt the larvae, a voracious insect, a defoliator of vegetation, a destroyer of crops.

A palmer is someone from the Holy Land who carries a palm leaf as a sign he has completed a pilgrimage.

Oddly enough, in the USA, the name Palmerworm is given to that defoliator of apple trees, the larva of the moth Ypsolophus pometellus. And in the 16th century a hairy caterpillar with wandering ways that destroyed vegetation was also called the palmerworm. It is seen in the Bible as a lesson to the unfaithful, part of God's judgement for losing faith in Him.

Locust

Reference to find:

The conies are but a feeble folk,
Yet make they their houses in the rocks;
*The **locusts** have no king,*
Yet go they forth all of them by bands;
The spider taketh hold with her hands,
And is in Kings' palaces.
Proverbs 30:26,27,28

If I shut up heaven that there be no rain,
*or if I command the **locusts** to devour the land.....*
2 Chronicles 7:13

Natural History Notes on the Locust, Locusta migratoria, an insect on the move.

Here in Britain and in Europe we do receive odd individuals from time to time but up to now they haven't been able to breed. Who knows how Climate Change may alter this? The Locust is a species of the Orthoptera, a large, highly gregarious grasshopper and a great plague in tropical and sub-tropical countries where it destroys vegetables and crops over wide areas. It migrates in huge swarms.

The Locust is undoubtedly the most important insect in the Bible and the only one allowed as food. Such were the swarms they blotted out the sun! They are the 8th plague yet as food were

eaten by John the Baptist. They are eaten today, without the head and legs, fried in butter.

The Locust lays her eggs in the ground and these develop into larvae that eat only green shoots. The next stage of development is the shedding of the skin to become a larger insect that can eat large amounts of vegetation and this is when most crop damage is done. The insect then develops short wings and tends to attack tree bark until the wings grow fully, the locust then being ready to migrate as well as mate and reproduce.

Along with grasshoppers they belong to the Acrididae Family but Locusts are capable of sustained flight hence the invasions of cultivated lands.

Locust *(Locusta migratoria)*

Caterpillar

Reference to find:

That which the palmerworm hath left hath the locust eaten;
and that which the locust hath left hath the cankerworm eaten;
*and that which the cankerworm hath left hath the **caterpillar** eaten.* Joel 1:4

Natural History Note on the Caterpillar

Thought now to refer to a stage in the development of the Locust, as is the Cankerworm.

Grasshopper

Reference to find:

*…also when they shall be afraid of that which is high, and fears shall be in the way, and the almond tree shall flourish,
and the* **grasshopper** *shall be a burden, and desire shall fail:* Ecclesiastes 12:5

Natural History Notes on the Grasshopper

Nine references to grasshoppers, all in the Old Testament refer to large numbers, small size and the fact they are permitted food.

Which grasshopper is the Bible Land insect? **Truxalis grandis** is sometimes mentioned by zoologists today. It is interesting that the song, or stridulation, differs from species to species and experts can tell which is which without seeing the actual insect.

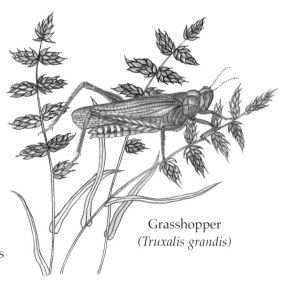

The true or Short-horned Grasshopper differ from Crickets and Bush Crickets in having short, thickish antennae instead of long thread-like ones. The British species are active by day. Males are generally smaller than females.

Grasshopper
(Truxalis grandis)

Eggs are laid in batches enclosed in strong egg pods and pass the winter in this stage. Nymphs hatch in Spring. Both they and the adults are entirely vegetarian, feeding mainly on grasses.

Gnat

Reference to find:

Ye blind guides, which strain at a **gnat***, and swallow a camel.* Matthew 23:24

Natural History Notes on the Gnat

The gnat is mentioned once only in Matthew, by Christ Himself, referring to the Jewish practice

Gnat *(Culex pipiens)*

of straining wine through cloth to remove insects.

In Britain and Europe the gnat is a small fly of the genus Culex, the **Common Gnat** being **Culex pipiens,** an abundant mosquito of stagnant water areas. There are 50 British species of the family Culicidae, many of them called gnats. Only the females pierce the skin of animals and suck blood.

In America gnat refers to **mosquitoes** and they are very common in Bible Lands today.

Moth

Reference to find:

Behold, the Lord God will help me; who is he that shall condemn me?
*lo, they all shall wax old as a garment; the **moth** shall eat them up.* Isaiah 50:9

Natural History Notes on the Moth

The Bible refers to moths as destructive insects and scholars plump for Clothes Moths of the family Tineidae as the garment and cloth destroyers of those times when no doubt clothing was precious and not so available as it is today.

The Clothes Moth
(Tineola bisselliella)

Our **Common Clothes Moth (Tineola bisselliella)** is found indoors in most parts of the British Isles and flies from June to September. Those seen are usually males, the females being more sedentary. However, it is not the moth but its larvae that does the damage, feeding usually from October to June on wool, fur and hair. They then pupate inside silken cocoons amongst their food.

Tineola, diminutive of Tinea, a clothes moth. Tinea, a gnawing worm, applied to the larvae. bisselliella, a seat of honour, from the larval occupancy of chair upholstery.

Fly

Reference to find:

*And it shall come to pass in that day, that the Lord shall hiss for the **fly** that is in the uttermost part of the rivers of Egypt, and for the bee that is in the land of Assyria.* Isaiah 7:18

Natural History Note on the Fly

Two references stand out in particular, one to a plague according to Psalms 78 and 105. Some species of biting midge is likely, or **mosquito**.

Mosquito *(Theobaldia annulata)*
(A British variety)

Flea

Reference to find:

*After whom is the king of Israel come out? after whom dost thou pursue? after a dead dog, after a **flea**.* 1 Samule 24:14

Natural History Note on the Flea

Probably the **human flea, Pulex irritans** which also parasitises other hole dwelling animals, bearing in mind man once lived in caves.

Flea *(Pulex irritans)*

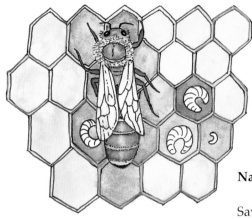

The Honey Bee
(*Apis Mellifera*)

Bees

References to find:

*They compassed me about like **bees**;* Psalm 118:12

Natural History Notes on Bees

Savage insects in the Bible Lands, protecting their honey against all who disturb them, yet providers of sweetness too. The insect is no doubt **Apis mellifera**, the **honey bee**, associated with humans for thousands of years.

Here it is almost entirely domesticated and even known as the Hive Bee. Occasionally along green shady riverbanks I find colonies living in hollow trees and there are always springtime swarms to keep an eye on. Enough food is stored in summer to keep a community alive in winter.

The community consists of drones (males) whose sole purpose is to fertilise the Queen. They die after doing so or are killed by the workers; a Queen (female) who lays eggs; and workers (sterile females).

The full story of the Honey Bee would fill this book and more, a world wide insect of renown.

Hornet

Reference to find:

*And I sent the **hornet** before you, which drave them out from before you, even the two kings of the Amorites;* Joshua 24:12

Natural History Notes on the Hornet

In the Bible an instrument of the punishment of God and referred to three times. **Vespa orientalis,** the **Oriental Wasp** fit's the bill nicely in Bible Lands although there were four species, two nesting in trees and two in cavities or underground.

Our **Hornet (Vespa crabro)** seems to be making a comeback after declining in numbers. Despite its large size it is the most docile of wasps if left to its own devices. It uses its fearsome sting on humans only if attacked. It nests in hollow trees and similar locations and will nest in nest boxes erected for birds. It is a tawny yellow social wasp more than 1in (2½ cms) long.

The females, but not the males, of all wasps have stings. Adults feed on nectar and fruit juices. Larvae feed on the bodies of other insects. Wasps have no pollen collecting organs.

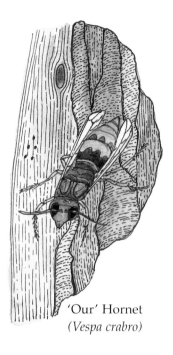

'Our' Hornet
(*Vespa crabro*)

Beetle

Reference to find:

*…. even these of them ye may eat; the locust after his kind, and the bald locust after his kind, and the **beetle** after his kind, and the grasshopper after his kind.* Leviticus 11:22

Natural History Note on the Beetle

One reference only (Lev 11.21-2) but all modern translators have opted for either Locust or Grasshopper.

The English Scarab *(Corpis lunaris)*
Very rare. A relative of the famous sacred Scarab Beetle worshipped by the Ancient Egyptians.

Spider

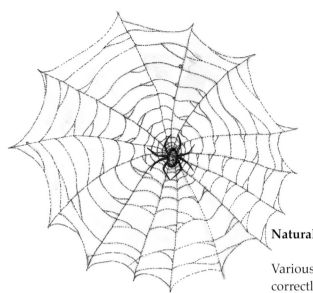

Whose hope shall be cut off,
*And whose trust shall be a **spider's web.*** Job 8:14

'Our' Garden Spider
(Araneus diadematus)

Natural History Notes on the Spider

Various spiders are common in Bible Lands and it is generally agreed most references are correctly referring to them. David's life was saved by a Spider when God had it spin a web over the entrance to the cave he was hiding in when pursued by Saul. Ironic in that David had earlier doubted God's wisdom in creating such a creature of no value. A lesson to all of us that there is reason in all living things even if we cannot fathom out why.

It is thought the 'spider' referred to in Proverbs that 'taketh hold with her hands, and is in King's palaces' is probably a gecko or lizard.

Lice

Reference to find:

And the Lord said unto Moses, Say unto Aaron, Stretch out thy rod, and smite the dust of the land,
*that it may become **lice** throughout all the land of Egypt.* Exodus 8:16

Natural History Notes on Lice

There are sucking lice and biting lice and that referred to in the Bible is said to be the **Human Louse, Pediculus humanus.** Those of us who recall 'bug nurses' visiting schools to check our heads and hair will know what a problem lice could become. Some have specialised in parts of the body, our 'head bug' being the sub-species **Pediculus humanus capitis** whereas another **P.h.humanus** is the body louse.

From a naturalists viewpoint lice are so specialised that some have helped identify relationships in bird groups.

The Human Louse are sucking lice of the Order Anoplura and are parasitic on mammals only. They normally attack no other species. The two varieties corporus, confined to the body, and capitis, mainly confined to the head, can interbreed. Females cement their 'nits' singly to the hairs or clothes of hosts. The nymphs hatch in a week or two, suck blood like the adults and mature in about 10 days.

Human Louse
(Pediculus humanus)

Human lice are found the world over where people live in crowded, unhygienic conditions particularly among children in crowded areas. They cause considerable irritation and can spread serious diseases including typhus and louse borne relapsing fever.

There are some 500 species of Bird Lice in Britain including the **chicken louse, Menopon gallinae** which is commonly found on poultry, and the **pigeon louse, Columbicola columbae** which lives amongst the feathers of pigeons and doves. They are of the Order Mallophaga.

Book lice are of the Order Psocoptera. The **Common Book Louse, Trogium pulsatorium** is found all over Britain and Europe in books, insect collections and foodstuffs, especially where damp occurs. They feed on paste used in book binding, some on paste used in wallpapering or on damp plastering in new properties, and are not actually lice at all.

Snail

Reference to find:

*As a **snail** which melteth, let every one of them pass away.* Psalm 58:8

Natural History Notes on the Snail

Psalm 58:8 refers to a snail and it is generally considered to be one of the genus Helix, 'as a snail which metteth.' In Bible Lands where limestone provides calcium for shells there are over 60 species of the family Helicidae alone.

Roman Snail
(Helix pomatia)

The Snail is a univalve mollusc of land and fresh water. Our largest species is the **Roman Snail, Helix pomatia**. Its close relative is the variable **Common or Garden Snail, Helix aspersa**, common in our gardens. It was once eaten in Britain as it still is on the Continent and is said to have once been sold in Bristol markets as 'wall fish'!

H.pomatia is widespread in Central Europe, extending westwards to C.France and S.E.England, and North to the S.Baltic Coasts. It has been introduced to Norway, Sweden and Finland.

H.aspersa is widespread in Britain, Belgium, Netherlands, W.Switzerland and W.Germany, East to the Rhine Valley.

Snails are mainly active at night or in wet weather due to the need to avoid drying up. After mating they lay eggs, usually in clutches in out of the way places such as beneath logs and stones. Egg numbers vary greatly, often 20-50 in large species but 100 or more in some. Rate of development depends on temperature but most hatch in about 6 weeks. More than one clutch may be laid in a season.

Young are like miniature adults, their development being direct. Young grow by adding to the leading edge of the shell, adding whorls as they grow.

Snails may be found in a variety if habitats, most in lime rich soil types.

Worm

Reference to find:

They shall lick the dust like a serpent, they shall move out of their holes like worms of the earth: Micah 7:17

Natural History Notes on the Worm

The Earthworm is commonly found in Bible Lands but none of the references to Worms in the Bible point clearly to them as such. It seems likely some references are to maggots, the larvae of various flies which swarm about rubbish but in Job, comments on dead bodies 'covering' and 'feeding sweetly' may relate to Earthworms.

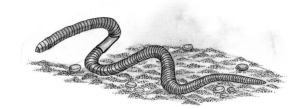

Earthworm
(Allolobophora longa)

Our commonest of 25 species often abundant in the soil are **Allolobophora longa** and **A.nocturna.** Our largest, and one of our commonest species is **Lumbricus terrestris** which can reach a foot (30cms) in length. The latter is known to anglers as dew worm, squirrel tail and twachel. It has a U shaped burrow from which it emerges at night while feeding on leaves and other decaying vegetable matter, plugging the entrance by day with twigs and leaves.

Segmented worms, including Earthworms are classified in the group Annelida.

Some Earthworms pass their food of decaying vegetable matter through their bodies, ejecting it on the surface as 'worm casts' consisting of soil-like organic refuse.

Horse Leech

Reference to find:

*The **horseleach** hath two daughters, crying, Give, give.* Proverbs 30:15

Natural History Notes on the Horse Leech

Leeches are external parasites that occur on land and in water. Common in Bible Lands it seems that some will attach themselves to the nostrils and mouths of horses when they are drinking. A decline in leeches followed the draining of swamp areas and the tapping of rivers but fish farms are now aiding a revival in some areas.

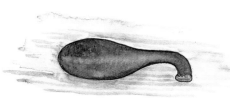

Horse Leech
(Haemopis sanquisuba)

The **Common Horse Leech (Haemopis sanquisuba)** feeds on frogs and fishes, not horses. The **Medicinal Leech**, the only one capable of piercing human skin is **Hirudo medicinalis,** now rare and apparently almost confined to the New Forest. There is a **Large Leech (Trocheta subviridis)** sometimes met with in country lanes and gardens close to water. The adults leave the water to hunt Earthworms in the soil.

Conclusion To The Natural History Notes
On Other Animals

Sadly we must accept that the wildlife of Biblical times is not all that it used to be. But that applies more or less across the planet. However, attempts are being made to right the wrongs and the Hai Bar Yotvata Reserve, in Israel, was set up in 1968, with the aims to reintroduce and acclimatize the desert animals of the Bible Lands. An area of about 3000 acres (12kms) was fenced and remarkable gains have been made.

There are tours for visitors to be found on the internet at the following address; http://www.kibbutzlotan.com/tourism/attractions/haibar.htm

Wild Ass, Addax, White Oryx, Ostrich and such are to be found in the area.

PART THREE

Introducing the Plants of the Bible

"And God said, Let the earth bring forth grass, the herb yielding seed, and the fruit tree yielding fruit after his kind, whose seed is in itself, upon the earth: and it was so." Genesis 1:11

"And God said, Behold I have given you every herb bearing seed, which is upon the face of all the earth, and every tree, in the which is the fruit of a tree yielding seed;" Genesis 1:29

Welcome to the last section of our "Celebration of Flora and Fauna of the Bible". We have by no means covered every species of flora and flora mentioned in the Bible but, I think it is fair to say that we have covered the majority.

Celebrating the plants of the Bible has been most interesting and the quote above from Genesis 1:29 really rings home to us that we were given, by God, the herbs and fruit trees to look after and use. Let us not let Him down. Even plants we can't use have a purpose for some creature or other. It is down to us to safe guard our own future by safe guarding what we can of the flora and fauna that was entrusted to us. Member's of Parliament are there for you, so if you are worried about loosing a wild habitat, or if some other threat to wildlife occurs, do write and ask that the wildlife is considered in their plans. With so many people needing homes, it is of course difficult to strike a balance for Nature, but it is not altogether impossible to achieve. There is always something one can do….

As before, Trevor Beer continues with his Natural History Notes and my chosen 'references to find', have been taken from the Authorised Version of the Bible unless otherwise indicated. Finally, as a special celebration, lets all plant a native tree for future generations to enjoy….

Aloe

Eaglewood
(Aquilaria agallocha)

References to find:

*"I have perfumed my bed
With myrrh, **aloes**, and cinnamon"*
Proverbs 7:17

*"And there came also Nicodemus, which at the first came to Jesus by night,
and brought a mixture of myrrh and **aloes**, about an hundred pound weight."*
John 19:39

The Natural History Notes on Aloe

The Aloes of the Old Testament are different from those of the New Testament. The former are a rare native tree from Burma and Assam **(Aquilaria agallocha)** known as **Eaglewood** whilst these of John are the true or bitter Aloes used as a spice for embalming the dead, **Aloe barbadense**.

Almond

Reference to find:

*"And their father Israel said unto them, If it must be so now, do this; take of the best fruits in the land in your vessels,
and carry down the man a present, a little balm, and a little honey, spices, and myrrh, nuts and **almonds**:"* Genesis 43:11

*"also when they shall be afraid of that which is high, and fears shall be in the way, and the **almond tree** shall flourish,
and the grasshopper shall be a burden, and desire shall fail:"* Ecclesiastes 12:5

The Natural History Notes on Almond

The Almond tree of Bible Lands may be seen in blossom as early as January and the Aaron's Rod of the Bible is the branch of the Almond and not the 'Aaron's Rod' wildflower of the British Isles.

It is closely related to the peach, apricot and nectarine and is **Prunus amygdalus (Rosaceae)**. It differs from them in that the soft husk is not edible and covers the kernel. Almonds have long been valued in the Near East for their oil.

It was regarded as the sacred tree of life over 1000 years before Christ was born. It is likely Almonds originated in western Asia but they have been planted in Mediterranean lands since ancient times and are naturalised in many areas.

Almonds are valued for their fruits, the kernels of which are used in confectionary or ground to make marzipan. The kernel of the bitter almond has to have its highly poisonous prussic acid removed before oil can be used for food flavouring.

In Britain **Prunus dulcis** is commonly grown, mainly for decoration and the blossom is an early indication of spring's coming. Usually our summers are too cold for the fruit to ripen fully but occasionally a hot summer will ripen it to release an oval, pitted nut containing an edible kernel. May grow to 30ft (9m).

Almond sprig
with fruit
(Prunus dulcis)

Apple

References to find:

"Who is this that cometh up from the wilderness,
Leaning upon her beloved?
*I raised thee up under the **apple tree**:*
There thy mother brought thee forth:
Song of Solomon 8:5

"A word fitly spoken
*Is like **apples** of gold in pictures of silver."*
Proverbs 25:11

The Natural History Notes on Apple

The Bible 'Apple' is not our common apple for certain. It is not a native of Palestine and wild apples are small, bitter and not particularly edible. Thus arguments as to the Old Testament fruit continue and oranges, though now one of Palestine's main exports were not around in 'Bible days.' The citron and the quince have been ruled out due to their bitter taste and we seem to be

'Our' Crab Apple
(*Malus sylvestris*)

left with the **Apricot**, one of the most abundant fruits of Bible Lands. Shady trees and sweet tasting fruit of the Song of Solomon link nicely with this delicious fruit, **Prunus armenaica** of the **Rosaceae** family.

In Britain, possibly from Continental Europe via Asia we have **Pyrus communis**, the **Common Pear** which originally came from Western Asia. Its fruits have been eaten in Europe for thousands of years.

It is **Malus sylvestris**, the **Crab Apple**, which is said to be the ancestor of all the cultivated apples of today with centuries of selection bringing about the major food and drink industry from the fruits. The Crab Apple recolonised Britain after the Ice Age and is thus regarded as a native tree. It is still to be found scattered throughout British oak woods. It has thorns.

Old country names for Crab Apple include Scrab, Bittersgall, Gribble, Scrogg, and Sour Grabs.

Crab Apple Jelly and Wine are delicious and a crab apple or two improve Apple Pie just as a quince does.

Aspalathus

Reference to find:

*"I gave a sweet smell like cinnamon and **aspalathus**, and I yielded a pleasant odour like the best myrrh, as galbanum, and onyx, and sweet storax, and as the fume of frankincense in the tabernacle"*
Ecclesiasticus 24:15 This quotation comes from The Apocrypha.

Natural History Notes on Aspalathus

A woody shrub with small, sharp thorns bearing beautifully perfumed flowers. The shrub provides **Lignum rhodianum**, an essence used by the ancients as a body perfume. It was also used as a hair and beard lotion and a purgative drug is extracted from the roots.

The plant is found growing well along North African shores and is found in the Canary Islands.

Balm

*"Is there no **balm** in Gilead; is there no physician there? Why then is not the health of the daughter of my people recovered?"*
Jeremiah 8:22

*"And they sat down to eat bread: and they lifted up their eyes and looked, and, behold,
a company of Ishmeelites came from Gilead with their camels bearing spicery and **balm** and myrrh, going to carry it down to Egypt."*
Genesis 37:25

The Natural History Notes On Balm

Balm (Balsam) a liquid gum flowing from a wounded Balsam tree. The Balm of Gilead tree (Jer) is a small evergreen with straggly branches. It is trained like a vine. Balsam, or Balm, is obtained from its stem, fruit and branches. **Commiphora gileadensis** or **C.opobalsamum**.

Some say Jeremiah's 'balm' which was medicinal and not necessarily fragrant was **Balanites aegyptiaca**, the **Jericho Balsam** found in the plains of Jericho and the rocky terrain of Gilead.

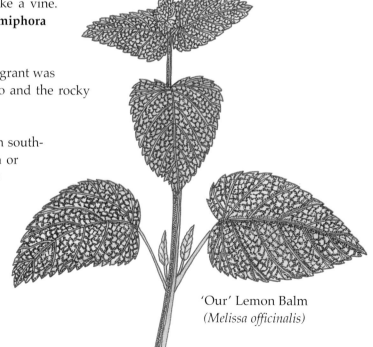

'Our' Lemon Balm
(*Melissa officinalis*)

The Balm we know is **Melissa officinalis**, a lovely herb introduced from southern and central Europe. The leaves have a lemon fragrance. Balm tea or cordial removes melancholy and cheers the heart and bees love it. Hives were rubbed with balm to keep the bees happy together and make others join them.

Balm comes via the French from the Latin balsamum, 'balsam'.

The Bible tells us "We hanged our harps upon the willows in the midst thereof" (Psalms) but this would have been the **poplar**, not the willow. **Populus euphratica** it is, growing well along shallow rivers from Syria to Palestine, Arabia, Petra and the Jordan Valley, one legend says it furnished the wood for the Cross of Jesus.

Barley

References to find:

*"So Naomi returned, and Ruth the Moabitess, her daughter in law, with her, which returned out of the country of Moab: and they came to Beth-lehem in the beginning of **barley** harvest.* Ruth 1:22

Natural History Notes on Barley

Barley is sown in Palestine in the autumn, through October and November and is harvested in spring during the Passover season. A second sowing may occur after winter. A bread was made from barley and was the Hebrews staple food though having a smaller protein content than wheat or rye, was more a symbol of poverty.

The bread of the five loaves and two fishes, feeding the multitudes, was barley bread.

Barley has been found in the Stone Age dwellings and Egyptian tombs.

(See wheat and rie.)

Six Row Barley
(Hordeum vulgare)

Bay

Reference to find:

*"I have seen the wicked in great power,
And spreading himself like a green **bay tree**."* Psalm 37:35

Natural History Notes on The Bay Tree

Herrings soused in vinegar, with **Bay** leaves, a mouth watering dish to be savoured and the Bay **(Laurus nobilis)** grows happily in our garden at home, as an attractive evergreen addition to the herb garden.

There is only one reference to it in the Bible, as a symbol of prosperity, and the tree is well known in Bible Lands. It has a delightful spicy fragrance and is a world renown condiment as well as the fruit, leaves, bark and roots all being used medicinally. The leaves are also used to produce a green oil known as 'Oil of Bay'.

Sweet Bay we call it, a tree sacred to the God Apollo. Originally it came from northern Asia but is now widely distributed throughout Europe and the Mediterranean, thriving in urban areas where it is resistant to pollution.

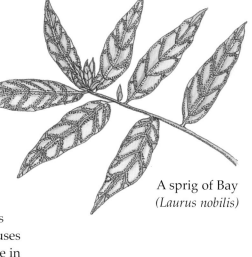

A sprig of Bay
(Laurus nobilis)

Its culinary uses are best known today as a meat flavouring or combined with other herbs as a general 'mixed spices' asset to the kitchen. Bay leaves were burnt to disinfect the air in houses and made cough medicines and a laxative. The large green oval berries turn black when ripe in late autumn. The tree may reach 10ft (3m) if not clipped back.

Beans

Reference to find:

*"…and Barzillai the Gileadite of Rogelim, brought beds, and basons, and earthen vessels, and wheat, and barley, and flour, and parched corn, and **beans**, and lentils,…"*
2 Samuel 17:28

Natural History Notes on Beans

Widely cultivated even today in Egypt and Syria, beans are a staple article of diet and sometimes mixed with flour to make bread. They are fed to horses and the stalks are fed to camels. The harvest is in June at the time of the wheat harvest.

White and black beans were used in ancient vote casting, the white to signify approval, the black a 'no', much the same as our own 'blackballing' of those who meet with our disapproval today.

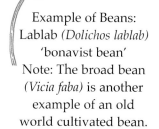

Example of Beans:
Lablab *(Dolichos lablab)*
'bonavist bean'
Note: The broad bean
(Vicia faba) is another
example of an old
world cultivated bean.

Box

References to find:

*"The glory of Lebanon shall come unto thee, the fir tree, the pine tree, and the **box** together, to beautify the place of my sanctuary;"*
Isaiah 60:13

Box *(Buxus longifolia)*

Natural History Notes on Box

Often referred to as a forest tree, it actually grows in the shade of other trees, keeping the ground shaded and cool and sheltering the fallen leaves. This prevents them blowing away, helping in their decomposition and return to the soil as food for forest trees as well as itself. The scientific name **Buxus longifolia** tells of its long leaves, longer than the European Box and for centuries the timber has been used for making musical instruments and for inlaying cabinet work. It grows in Lebanon and the Galilean hills and is found in the Mediterranean region.

Sprigs of **Box** have been found in England in tombs dating from the Roman occupation.

Bramble

Reference to find:

*"Then said all the trees unto the **bramble**, Come thou, and reign over us.*
*And the **bramble** said unto the trees, If in truth ye anoint me king over you,*
then come and put your trust in my shadow: and if not,
*let fire come out of the **bramble** and devour the Cedars of Lebanon."* Judges 9:14, 15

Natural History Notes on Bramble

What a joy to come home purple-fingered, with fresh summer blackberries ready for blackberry and apple pie. I did so as a lad and do so now, aware though to leave plenty for birds and other wildlife. I have watched foxes delicately picking and eating blackberries whilst pheasants strut quite unconcernedly close by them!

The **Bramble** of Bible Lands is said to be our very same **Blackberry** bush though it should be remembered we have about 400 species in Britain alone.

Rubus ulmifolius is mentioned by some botanists though our Bramble is **Rubus fruticosus** today with over 2,000 varieties or micro-species recorded in the Rubii family. One only has to examine the obvious differences in both flowers and fruit on many a bush to realise they are not one and the same, even in small areas at times.

Though the reference to Bramble in Luke does not say so, Folklore tells us the Devil spits on blackberries after Michaelmas Day (29th Sept). Actually it is a flesh fly which does so, dribbling its saliva onto the fruits, then sucking up the juices more easily. Thus it is sound advice to leave well alone beyond that date.

See how the arching stems push into the ground to form new plants.

Old country names include Mushes, Yeo-Brimmel, Country Lawyers, Black Kites, Hawk's Bill Bramble, Doctor's Medicine, and Brier.

It is said Christ switched the donkey on the way to Jerusalem with a blessed bramble, then drove the moneylenders out of the temple.

In Cornwall a charm using 9 bramble leaves and the purification of spring water goes….
There came three angels out of the east,
One brought fire and two brought frost.
Out fire and in frost,
In the name of the Father, Son and Holy Ghost.

The Bramble showing
flowers and fruit
(*Rubus fruticosus*)

Brier

References to find:

*"Instead of the thorn shall come up the fir tree, and instead of the **brier** shall come up the myrtle tree:…"* Isaiah 55:13

*"And there shall be no more a pricking **brier** unto the house of Israel, nor any grieving thorn of all that are round about them, that despised them; and they shall know that I am the Lord God."* Ezekiel 28:24

Natural History Notes on Brier

More translation 'fun' with a number of prickly plants of the Bible translated into English as Thorns, Briers, Brambles, Thistles, and Nettles. Much of the desert habitat plants are prickly, and flourish in such conditions. The Brier of Isaiah and Micha is said to be the **Palestinian Nightshade** or **Jericho Potato, Solanum incanum,** found commonly in the valley of the Jordan and around the Dead Sea.

Nightshades of Britain include two beautiful plants. One, **Solanum dulcamara**, or **Bittersweet (Woody Nightshade)** is found in many a wood and hedgerow flowering from June through September. Its blue-purple flowers light the greenery and young green fruits turn yellow, then red. It is a climber of other shrubs and vegetation but adopts a sprawling habit over the ground where there are no support plants.

Brier:
Bittersweet
(Solanum dulcamara)

'dulcamara' is from two Latin words meaning sweet and bitter, hence its common English name. The toxic alkaloid solanine is present in the stem, leaves and berries and they taste bitter at first then sweet.

Black Nightshade, Solanum nigrum, is common in England, but rarer in Wales and almost absent from Scotland. It is an upright non-climbing plant with blue-green leaves and tiny, drooping white flowers, very pretty in cultivated areas and doing well in urban sites.

Solanum means solace and refers to the plant's medicinal properties despite it containing solanine. Leaves were used for compresses to ease the pain of boils and burns and their juice made an excellent mouthwash. Both plants are native to the British Isles.

Potatoes and aubergines are close relatives.

Brier, in Britain refers to Bramble. Briar refers to the Wild or Dog Rose.

Bulrush

References to find:

*"And when she could not longer hide him, she took for him an ark of **bulrushes**, and daubed it with slime and with pitch, and put the child therein; and she laid it in the flags by the river's brink."* Exodus 2:3

*"… that sendeth ambassadors by the sea, even in vessels of **bulrushes** upon the waters,…"* Isaiah 18:2

Natural History Notes on Bulrush

Bulrushes, or Reedmace, waving brown velvet heads over rippling marsh water as a moorhen swims the reed fringe with her fluffy ink black young….

A typical English freshwater marsh scene but as we make our natural history notes do we remember the Bulrush is the papyrus of paper making?

Moses in the Bulrushes, a papyrus basket holding the infant, a delightful Bible tale and of course the Greeks it was who called the white pith inside the stems byblos and the books made from it bybla, hence the word 'Bible'.

The Papyrus has smooth three angled stems and can reach 10ft (3m) or more ending in a plume of grass-like stalks each bearing clusters of little brown flower heads. More of a sedge really.

Our **Bulrush** is **Typha latifolia**, the Greater Bulrush and there is a **Lesser**, **Typha augustifolia**, both rising from thick underwater roots. The female flower of the Greater Bulrush is about 6ins (15cms) long or more and has thousands of tighly packed flowers. Flowers June and July.

The seeds were once used to stuff mattresses, and baskets and chairs were woven from the leaves. As the leaves are waterproof reed boats were made from them.

It was the popularity of the painting 'Moses in the bulrushes' by Alma-Tadema, showing **Typha latifolia** in error that formed our mental picture of the bulrush.

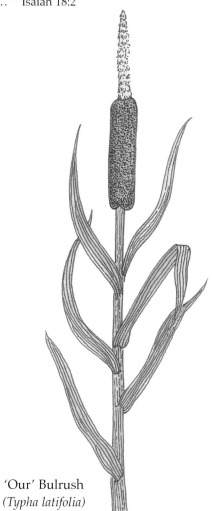

'Our' Bulrush
(Typha latifolia)

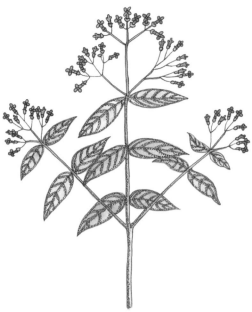

Henna in fruit
(*Lawsonia inermis*)

Camphire

References to find:

*"Thy plants are an orchard of pomegranates, with pleasant fruits;
Camphire, with spikenard,…"* Song of Solomon 4:13

Natural History Notes on Camphire

The Camphire of the Song of Solomon is actually **henna (Lawsonia inermis)** also known as **Egyptian Privet**. It is still common in some areas such as Engedi on the Dead Sea just a few miles north of Herod's fortress at Masada, as it was in Solomon's days.

Henna was used to stain the skin and nails of Egyptian mummies. The Children of Israel used it cosmetically but Jewish leaders objected to the cosmetic uses as being pagan in spirit.

It is a tropical shrub with many small, white highly perfumed flowers which hang in drupe clusters.

Cassia

Reference to find:

*"Dan also and Javan going to and fro occupied in thy fairs: bright iron,
cassia, and calamus, were in thy market."* Ezekiel 27:19

Natural History Notes on Cassia

The **Cassia** of the Psalms is **Saussurea lappa**, the **Indian orris**, from the Himalayas. It was used as an aphrodisiac, a perfume, and medicinally. The roots are fragrant.

The Cassia of Exodus and Ezekial is the Cassia-bark tree, Cinnamomum cassia, from Ceylon and the Far East. (See cinnamon)

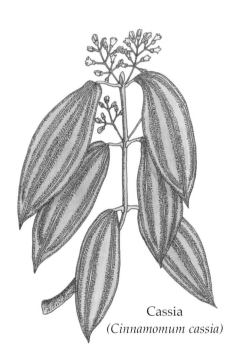

Cassia
(*Cinnamomum cassia*)

Cedar of Lebanon

References to find:

*"The trees of the Lord are full of sap; The **Cedars of Lebanon,** which he hath planted;"* Psalm 104:16

*"They have made all thy ship boards of fir trees of Senir: they have taken **cedars** from **Lebanon** to make masts for thee."* Ezekiel 27:5

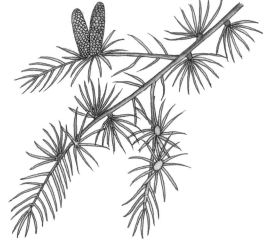

Natural History Notes on the Cedar of Lebanon

The greatest tree of Bible Lands, capable of reaching 120ft (40m) with a girth of 40ft (13m) it is a symbol of strength. Cedar is actually from the Arabic Kedra which means strength. It grows in the mountains of Asia Minor and the Lebanon and once formed vast forests covering the mountains, yet few remain today.

It is **Cedrus libani (Loudon)** a native of Mount Lebanon in Syria and was introduced into Britain about the year 1683. The simple leaves are very dense, about 30 to a tuft. Branches are horizontal, with branchlets disposed in a flat, fan-like manner thickly set with leaves.

In 1860 Hooker found the ancient Cedar forests of Lebanon to consist of nine groups of cedars amounting to about 400 in all. He estimated their ages as varying from 100 to 2500 years.

The Cedar of Lebanon
(Cedrus libani)

Cypress

Reference to find:

*"He heweth him down cedars, and taketh the **cypress** and the oak, which he strengtheneth for himself among the trees of the forest: he planteth an ash, and the rain doth nourish it."* Isaiah 44:14

Natural History Notes on the Cypress

Only one mention in the Bible, in Isaiah and there are two forms, one with spreading branches

reminiscent of a Cedar, the common form in its wild state, and the other an upright, erectly branched tree, almost parallel to the trunk and thus forming a triangular or pyramidal shape.

The cypress may grow very tall, the spreading form distributed throughout the northern range of mountains in Cyprus. It was abundant in Crete on the White mountains where it is said the snow never melts. The upright variety is cultivated all over Syria and known as Saru.

True Cypresses are known by their scale-like adpressed adult leaves, never in two ranks, monoecious flowers, male flowers spiked, anthers four or more, crested, pollen globose; cones globular or oblong, woody, ripening in second year. All species exude resin but no turpentine.

An Example of
Cypress

Chestnut

Reference to find:

*"And Jacob took him rods of green poplar, and of the hazel and **chestnut tree**;
and pilled white strakes in them, and made the white appear which was in the rods.* Genesis 30:37

Natural History Notes on The Chestnut

Awkward translations again! It seems the 'Hazel' of Genesis is the Almond and the Palestine 'Chestnut' is not indigenous so the Hebrew 'armon' means the **Oriental Plane Tree, (Platanus orientalis).** Truly the Plane does grow beside Palestine's streams and rivers whereas the Common Chestnut prefers hilly, dry situations.

The Plane tree was one of the first exotic trees to be introduced into Europe.

The well known **London Plane tree (Platanus X hispanica)** is a hybrid twixt the American or Western Plane and the Eastern or Oriental Plane. It is a natural hybrid now thriving in the city and elsewhere. They grow to about 100ft (30m) and are hardy with a domed crown and thick twisting branches. The fruits do not drop but

The Oriental Plane
(Platanus orientalis)

remain on the trees during winter which helps their popularity in streets and avenues. Americans refer to the tree as **Buttonwood**. The tree periodically sheds its bark which renders the trunk and branches with a smooth, naked look, which tends to confirm the Biblical 'Chestnut' was in fact a plane tree.

It is a majestic tree, called **Dulb** in Iranian and has been in cultivation in the Mediterranean region for centuries. It is indigenous in Crete, Cyprus and Rhodes and in Western and Southern Asia to 5000ft (1650m) with records of 30ft (10m) circumference and more. Pliny wrote of a Plane Tree and the hollow in its trunk measuring 81ft (27m).

and in comparison…
'our' Horse Chestnut tree
(*Aesculus hippocastanum*)

Cinnamon

Reference to find:

*"…and iron, and marble, and **cinnamon**, and odours, and ointments, and frankincense, and wine, and oil…"* Revelations 18:13

Natural History Notes on Cinnamon

The cinnamon is one of the oldest known spices and that which we have in Britain, from Sri Lanka, is considered the true Cinnamon and should not be confused with Cassia of North America.

Cinnamon was valued highly as a spice and a perfume and was one of the 'holy oil' ingredients of Moses.

It is a member of the Laurel family, growing to a height of 30ft (10m) or so, recognisable by its leaves which are beautifully veined. Cinnamon is actually obtained from the inner bark, quills being cut from the bark and tied in bundles.

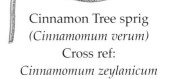

Cinnamon Tree sprig
(*Cinnamomum verum*)
Cross ref:
Cinnamomum zeylanicum

Note: The laurel so well known as a hedge plant in Britain is **Cherry Laurel (Prunus laurocerasus)** and not a true laurel. Introduced here in 1576 from S.E Europe it is hardy and grows on most soils except chalk. It was planted as game cover so is often found in old woods, growing to 20ft (18m) and was used as part of the amateur naturalists equipment, the leaves crushed into 'killing' jars by butterfly collectors. They contain prussic acid or cyanide, and smell of bitter almonds. Cherry Laurel from the round berries which are red at first, ripening to shiny black. It belongs to the same family as Almond and Plum (Rosaceae), and is sometimes known as Portuguese Laurel.

Cockle

Reference to find:

"Let thistles grow instead of wheat,
*And **cockle** instead of barley."* Job 31:40

Corn cockle
(*Agrostemma githago*)

Natural History Notes on Cockle

From the Book of Job and another dilemma for translators who considered Bramble, Dwarf Elder, Poppies, and White Aconite but eventually plumped for the **Common Corncockle** of cornfields, wheat and barley.

Corncockle, Agrostemma githago, has red-purple flowers which are solitary, with undivided petals. It was a common cornfield weed in Britain, the seeds becoming mixed with corn and lowering the quality of flour. It is now becoming a scarce plant due to so-called improved agricultural techniques. Corncockle flowers from June to August and grows to a height of 12-40ins (30-100cms). It is a beautiful wildflower still gracing a few field edges in the British countryside.

The ancient weed from Southern Europe is in decline. An old name, **Indian Herb** suggests its love of warmth and in France it is known as **God's Eye**, or **Christ's Eye**.

Old country names include Little and Pretty, Popple, Puck Needles, Robin Hood and Crown of the Field.

Puck is the goblin also known as Robin Goodfellow and Puck Needles refers to the long teeth of the calyx tube which spread out between the bright petals.

Coriander

Reference to find:

*"And the house of Israel called the name thereof Manna: and it was like **coriander** seed, white; and the taste of it was like wafers made with honey."* Exodus 16:31

Natural History Notes on Coriander

One of the Umbelliferae **(Coriandrum sativum)** mentioned twice only in the Bible and connected with 'manna'. What manna is we still do not know for certain, a tantalising puzzle but a food of life it was, much needed when the Children of Israel moaned at the lack of food following their escape from captivity.

Coriander is a wonderful herb, with parsley-like leaves, and its leaves and fruit very aromatic. The Children of Israel thought manna was like the coriander seed in shape, and bdellium in colour and we know bdellium was found in the Garden of Eden. (Genesis 2:12). It is a gum resin found in two species of commiphora, one African, one Indian, so the Garden of Eden's location is partly our choice. I think Africa, of the two.

Coriander leaves are used as in ancient times to flavour soups, puddings and wines. It is a member of the carrot family and all parts of the plant may be used. Seeds were found in the tombs of the pharaohs and are used today to flavour gin and as an ingredient in pickling spices. Use the fresh leaves sparingly as the taste tends to dominate. Used as an aphrodisiac. The seeds are essential ingredients in an Indian Curry, and an indispensable addition to the native chillis of Mexico and Peru. Excellent with fresh mint and cumin.

I have this very day just had a glass of red mulled wine with coriander in it, wonderful!

Coriander *(Coriandrum sativum)*

Cucumber

*"We remember the fish, which we did eat in Egypt freely; the **cucumbers**, and the melons, and the leeks, and the onions, and the garlick:"*

Numbers 11:5

Cucumber plant
(Cucumis sativus)

Natural History Notes on the Cucumber

They ate well in Egypt! Fish, cucumbers, melons, leeks, onions and garlic. Cucumbers probably originated in southern Asia.

Fields of cucumbers, with watchmen protecting them. Today cucumbers still grow aplenty in Egypt and Palestine and feature as important in the people's diet with all towns and villages selling them. They tend to be **Cucumber, Cucumis sativus,** flowering in summer and eaten as a salad vegetable for well over 3000 years.

Modern uses include the juice as part of many natural beauty creams and other cosmetics. As a beauty aid slices of Cucumber can be applied directly to the skin. The juice is also good against kidney ailments and rheumatic conditions especially if combined with carrot juice.

Usually eaten raw, they can be used in soups, or fried, or boiled and served in white sauce.

Ebony

Reference to find:

*"The men of Dedan were thy merchants; many isles were the merchandise of thine hand: they brought thee for a present horns of ivory and **ebony**."* Ezekiel 27:15

Natural History Notes on Ebony

Only one reference in the Bible, old Ezekiel again, surely one of the most interesting Books, and characters.

Ebony (Diospyros ebenum or **D.ebenaster)** We all know Ebony as the hard, black wood of piano keys and far more wonderful things and it is the interior wood, or heartwood, which is hard, heavy, black and valuable, the sapwood of the Ebony tree being soft, white and valueless.

Ebony and ivory were worked together as if created for each other and it has to be said, some of the results were and are amazing.

Egyptian statues of gods and goddesses representing night and darkness were carved from Ebony.

Ebony comes from the Hebrew eben, a stone and the name Ebenezer means 'stone of my help'. Dickens must have known that when writing of stony old Ebenezer Scrooge methinks.

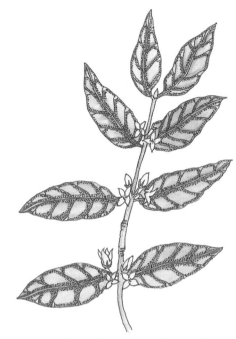

Ebony *(Diospyros ebenaster)*

Fig Tree

Reference to find:

*"…he was hungry: and seeing a **fig tree** afar off having leaves, he came, if haply he might find any thing thereon: and when he came to it, he found nothing but leaves; for the time of **figs** was not yet."* Mark 11:13

Natural History Notes on the Fig Tree

We had a huge fig tree in our garden when I was a lad and it fruited very well. It grew beside a large outhouse-cum-shed and I loved to use both as my den away from the house.

The **Fig Tree (Ficus carica)** is peculiar in that the fruit is not really a fruit at all, it is a large, fleshy and hollow receptacle which contains the flowers. Its fruit bearing can be a bit unreliable and in Matthew, Christ got a bit stroppy on finding a Fig Tree with no fruit, so he cursed it. Not much of a gardener it would seem.

In the Bible Lands the fig, vine and olive are the most important fruit trees.

Fig *(Ficus carica)*

The Fig is probably a native of Western Asia, widespread in warm temperate and sub-tropical regions. It can be self sown and naturalised even as far north as the British Isles. In addition to their food value, (they contain some 50% sugar when dried) they also have mild laxative properties and Syrup of Figs is well known medicinally and recommended in the British Pharmaceutical codex. Dried, tinned and preserved figs are very popular today.

The Fig Tree is a deciduous plant growing to about 30ft (10m) and belongs to the Mulberry family (Moraceae). In its countries of origin it is pollinated by a fig wasp but in Britain, as the Fig wasp does not occur here, the Fig Tree is able to fruit without being pollinated. The term for this is parthenocarpic, and applies also to dandelions and the hawkweeds.

(See Sycamore).

Flax

References to find:

*"But she had brought them up to the roof of the house, and hid them with the stalks of **flax**, which she had laid in order upon the roof."* Josh 2:6

*"For their mother hath played the harlot: she that conceived them hath done shamefully: for she said, I will go after my lovers, that give me my bread and my water, my wool and my **flax**, mine oil and my drink."* Hosea 2:5

Fairy Flax
(Linum catharticum)

Natural History Notes on Flax

Flax (Linum usitatissimum) waving gently in fields of misty blue is often a feature of the British countryside, an annual which crops well. Used for linen in Bible Lands, and for Linseed Oil, it is the world's most ancient textile plant and grown in Egypt long before the Israelites reached that country.

In Britain there are three native species. The commonest, the white flowered **Fairy** or **Purging Flax (L.catharticum),** the two others blue flowered and local in their distribution. They are difficult to find but **Cultivated Flax** is a frequent casual or escape from cultivation.

Fairy Flax has a gentle, fairy-like appearance and has attracted names such as Lady's Flax and Lady's Lint but when the bruised stems were simmered in wine to be used as a purgative the effects could be so violent it had to be discontinued.

Pale Flax (L.bienne) is one of the two blue species and found along our West Coasts of England and Wales in grassy places.

Perennial Flax (L.perenne ssp anglicum) has a darker blue flower and blooms from May through August.

Linen was the best known clothing material for thousands of years until ousted by mass-produced cotton in the 19th century. Today linen is used for higher quality cloth whilst linseed oil is used in some human foods and commonly in cattle cake. The purified oil is used in some paint and varnish products and putty.

Garlic (*Allium sativum*)

Garlick

Reference to find:

*"We remember the fish, which we did eat in Egypt freely; the cucumbers, and the melons, and the leeks, and the onions, and the **garlick**:"* Numbers 11:5

Natural History Notes on Garlick

We are told that **Garlick** was one of the vegetables missed by the Israelites on their way to the Promised Land. Garlic grew in abundance in Egypt and was one of the staple foods there. There are a number of species. **Garlic, leeks,** and **onions** helped feed the Egyptians building the pyramids, the Egyptians placing it among their deities.

Grape Vine

Reference to find:

*"In those days saw I in Judah some treading wine presses on the Sabbath, and bringing in sheaves, and lading asses;
as also wine, **grapes**, and figs, and all manner of burdens, which they brought into Jerusalem on the Sabbath day:
and I testified against them in the day wherein they sold victuals."* Nehemiah 13:15

Natural History Notes on the Grape Vine

Constant references in the Bible to Grape Vines, grapes and the wine made from them,
old Noah getting drunk from it. The Promised Land was a land of wheat, barley and
vines and fig trees (Deut).

The grape vine is the first cultivated plant mentioned in the Bible and it is thought
it originated in Armenia where wild grapes still grow abundantly, climbing trees
and producing masses of fruit without the aid of humans.

In Britain it has been a greenhouse plant for years but some success with outdoor
varieties and the thought that Climate Change will warm the British Isles up has had
speculators contemplating more British wine success recently.

Grape Vine sprig
(Vitis vinifera)

Hazel

Reference to find:

*"And Jacob took him rods of green poplar, and of the **hazel** and chestnut tree;
and pilled white strakes in them, and made the white appear which was in the rods.* Genesis 30:37

Natural History Notes on the Hazel Tree

Hazel in woods and hedgerows, lambs tail catkins herald the spring, the hedge nuts or cob nuts speaking of autumn, a wonderful tree in the British Isles.

In the Bible Hazel is mentioned as early as Genesis but modern translators say the reference is really to the **Almond**, though **Hazel (Corylus avellana)** does grow in the Near East as well as in Britain and Europe, especially along with oaks.

Old uses in Britain include coracle making going back more than 3,000 years, a boat much used by Welsh fisherman with a basket-like frame covered by animal hides. It is a magical tree in Britain.

A building method known as Wattle and Daub had hazel panels or wattles placed between wooden posts to form a house framework and then daubed with mud and straw. Similar undaubed panels are made to pen sheep to this day and known as hurdles.

'Double' Hazel nuts carried in the pocket keep toothache at bay - toothache obtained from cracking hazel nuts with ones teeth probably!

Old country names include Halse, Cobbedy Cut, Nuttall, and Filbeard.

Hazel Tree
(Corylus avellana)

Hemlock

References to find:

"They have spoken words, swearing falsely in making a covenant:
*thus judgement springeth up as **hemlock** in the furrows of the field."* Hosea 10:4

"Shall horses run upon rock? will one plow there with oxen?
*for ye have turned judgement into gall, and the fruit of righteousness into **hemlock**:"* Amos 6:12

Natural History Notes on Hemlock

Hemlock is a very beautiful member of the Parsley family which includes Wild Carrot and Parsnip but instead of the useful 'food for free' attributes of those two popular plants, Hemlock is poisonous and not to be toyed with.

Hemlock (Conium maculatum) is the Bible Hemlock and our own and is Biblically a symbol of misfortune, a grim plant in its way but no doubt good for some things.

In ancient Greece it was used as a death penalty just as hanging and the electric chair were used as the ultimate punishments in some countries.

Socrates the Greek philosopher ended his days having to drink a cup of Hemlock for what were judged his sins.

All parts of the plant are poisonous but the seeds particularly so, containing high concentrations of coniine. Thankfully the plant is easily identifiable by its smooth stems with their purple blotches, and an unpleasant, foetid smell. It grows to about 5ft (150cm) tall and has fern-like leaves and tiny white flowers in umbels. Flowers June to July.

Old country names include Devil's Blossom, Gipsy Flower, Cartwheel, Honiton Lace, Nosebleed and Stink Flower.

An alarming fact is that if Asses eat a lot of Hemlock they fall so fast asleep they may appear dead!

Hemlock
(Conium maculatum)

Hyssop

Reference to find:

"And he spake of trees, from the cedar tree that is in Lebanon even unto the **hyssop** *that springeth out of the wall:"* 1 Kings 4:33

Natural History Notes on Hyssop

More confusion with translations, possibly more so than any other botanical reference in the Bible.

Our garden **Hyssop** is the well known herb **(Hyssopus officinalis)** indigenous to southern Europe. It is said to be unknown in Bible Lands though Solomon, who spoke of Hyssop springing 'out of the wall', imported many animals and plants. Translators have suggested **Prickly**

Caper, Pokeweed, **Rue** and **White Marjoram** as 'hyssops', an interesting and confusing collection.

Hyssop and Marjoram are members of the Mint family, the Labiatae, and the **Syrian** or **White Marjoram (Origanum maru)** is a favourite choice to fit most of the scriptures referring to Hyssop. Growing up to 3ft (1m) or so in good soil the stems hold water and were used as sprinklers in religious ceremonies.

Our **Marjoram** is **(Origanum vulgare)** a perennial with an aromatic scent and purple flowers though I have seen white forms. It is common in hedge banks and dry fields and is grown in herb gardens.

Interestingly our Hyssop with its purplish flowers and aromatic narrow pointed leaves has a taste of rue within its own flavour, naturally of mint. In our garden it looks lovely and attracts bees and butterflies. Indeed it attracts the large and small white butterflies we call 'cabbage whites' so is a good companion plant to grow alongside cabbages and will attract these two insects away from our crops. It flowers from June to September.

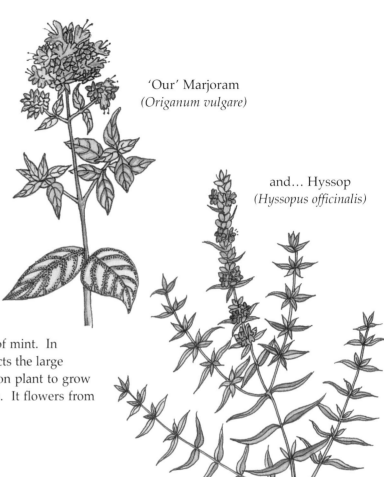

'Our' Marjoram
(*Origanum vulgare*)

and… Hyssop
(*Hyssopus officinalis*)

Juniper

Reference to find:

*"But he himself went a day's journey into the wilderness, and came and sat down under a **juniper tree**:"* 1 kings 19:4

*"Who cut up mallows by the bushes, And **juniper** roots for their meat."* Job 30:4

Natural History Notes on Juniper

In some versions of the Bible, Juniper is said to be broom. However, **Juniper (Retama raetum)** grows in Bible Lands and is one of the few plants offering shade in some desert regions. The Holy Family sheltered under a juniper tree.

'Our' Sprig of Juniper
(Juniperus communis)

Psalms 120 mentions 'coals of juniper' and the plant was used as charcoal and as firewood and burns very well. The ancient Egyptians used cedar oil made from juniper leaves which are aromatic, in mummification. This lends credence to the Biblical plant being a Juniper. In Medieval Europe juniper was burnt to keep away evil spirits and to help preserve smoked hams. Talking of spirits, juniper berries are used to flavour gin and in Holland the geneva drink equivalent. Where Hemlock is not good for us as far as we yet know, Juniper is good and the berries are used to produce a brown dye as well as medicinally against savage beasts, the plague and as an antidote to poison. Interestingly an acquaintance of mine who drinks copious amounts of gin was bitten by an adder on Dartmoor and barely noticed any symptoms! It Works!

'Our' **Juniper** is **Juniperus communis,** a native conifer growing naturally in a variety of situations. I found lots of it on Scottish hillsides flourishing on acid soils. Dwarf forms are popular for rock gardens. May grow to 20ft (6m) tall.

Juniper sauce is very nice with steaks.

Old country names include Bastard Killer, Horse Saving and Melmot Berries. A Scottish name is **Aiten**.

Even if the Biblical Juniper is in reality a type of **Broom**, as some translators say, we should not discount the possibility of a juniper for both **Chinese Juniper (Juniperus chinensis)** and the **Pencil Cedar** assume tree form. Hybrids are common.

Lentil

References to find:

*"Then Jacob gave Esau bread and pottage of **lentiles**; and he did eat and drink, and rose up, and went his way:"* Genesis 25:34

"And after him was Shammah the son of Agee the Hararite.
*And the Philistines were gathered together into a troop, where was a piece of ground full of **lentiles**:"* 2 Samuel 23:11

Natural History Notes on Lentil

Lentil (Lens esculenta) of the Leguminosae Family and one of the favourite Old Testament vegetables and a food for hungry peasants and herdsmen. The Lentil has always been in Bible Lands and is a small vetch-like annual borne in pea-like pods. In fact lentil is a member of the pea and bean family and said to be very nutritious, good for bone, muscle, nerve and brain tissue.

Lens culinaris we call the Lentil and it can be grown in the British Isles given a warm, light soil. It is believed to have originated in the Near East or the Mediterranean Region and is still grown commercially in those areas.

The seed shape is indicated by the name of the genus, Lens, from which the English word 'Lens' is taken. The commercial lentil is usually orange or reddish.

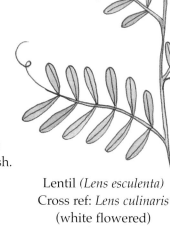

Lentil (*Lens esculenta*)
Cross ref: *Lens culinaris*
(white flowered)

Lily of the Valley

Reference to find:

"I am the rose of Sharon
*And the **lily of the valleys.**"*
Song of Solomon 2:1

Natural History Notes on Lily of the Valley

The English Lily of the Valley grows wildly beautiful in a woodland not far from my home and first blooms in late April or May. It is popular in gardens and has been cultivated for well over 500 years as lovely ground cover in shady areas. The flowers have a delightful scent, attractive to insects, and given to soaps and perfumes. This is **Convallaria majalis**, also used for eye inflammations medicinally and to strengthen the brain according to 16th century herbalist John Gerard.

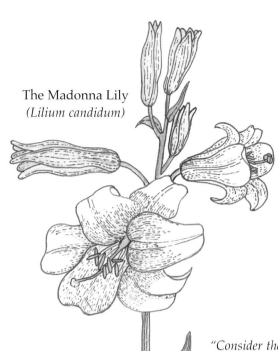

The Madonna Lily
(Lilium candidum)

However, this is not Lily of the Valley in Biblical terms, for 'ours' is unknown in Bible Lands so the translators vote goes to the **Common Hyacinth (Hyacinthus orientalis),** and the **Madonna Lily (Lilium candidum)** for both are still to be found in the regions.

Lilies of the Field

Reference to find:

*"Consider the **lilies** how they grow: they toil not, they spin not; and yet I say unto you that Solomon in all his glory was not arrayed like one of these."* Luke 12:27

Natural History Notes on Lillies of the Field

'Consider the lillies of the field, how they grow,' part of the well known verse of Luke, Chapter 12.

Almost certainly the **Poppy Anemone (Anemone coronaria)** of the Ranunculaceae family which still covers the ground in springtime in Bible Lands and is known as the Palestine anemone. It is even known as the Windflower just as our own white Wood Anemone is, but the Biblical Lilly of the Field is red.

Poppy Anemone
(Anemone coronaria)

Mallows

*"Who cut up **mallows** by the bushes, And juniper roots for their meat."* Job 30:4

Natural History Notes on Mallows

Not the true mallows of the Genus Malva, the **common mallow** we know so well, from its rose-purple flowers that grows so widely along our roadsides, or the **small musk mallow**, but a species of **saltwort** growing by the sea. It is a bushy shrub related to spinach, picked for its food value.

Mallow:
Saltwort
(*Atriplex halimus*)

Mandrake

References to find:

*"And Reuben went in the days of wheat harvest, and found **mandrakes** in the field, and brought them unto his mother Leah."* Genesis 30:14

Natural History Notes on Mandrake

This is **Mandragora officinarum**, one of the Solonaceae family, the potatoes, and related to the tomato. It is a harmless enough plant but because its roots resemble a man's reproductive areas, shall we say, it gained a reputation as an aphrodisiac.

It flowers early in the year and has fruits like small eggs on the ground amongst large dark green wrinkly leaves. The yellow flowers have purple veins like those of the potato. It is a native of the eastern Mediterranean and is also known as the love apple. It flowers from mid to late summer.

It should not be confused with the so-called English or American **Mandrakes, Bryonia dioica** and **Podophyllum peltatum** respectively.

Mandrake
(*Mandragora officinarum*)

Melon

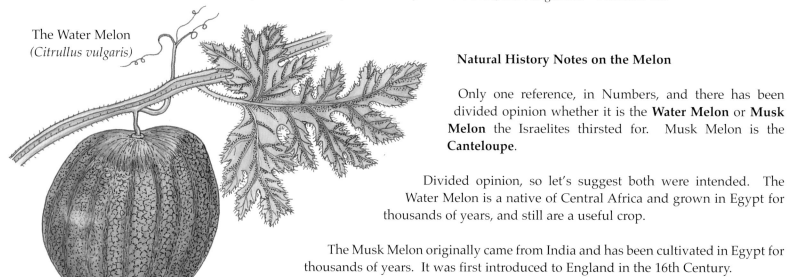

Reference to find:

*"We remember the fish, which we did eat in Egypt freely;
the cucumbers, and the **melons**, and the leeks, and the onions, and the garlick:"* Numbers 11:5

The Water Melon
(Citrullus vulgaris)

Natural History Notes on the Melon

Only one reference, in Numbers, and there has been divided opinion whether it is the **Water Melon** or **Musk Melon** the Israelites thirsted for. Musk Melon is the **Canteloupe**.

Divided opinion, so let's suggest both were intended. The Water Melon is a native of Central Africa and grown in Egypt for thousands of years, and still are a useful crop.

The Musk Melon originally came from India and has been cultivated in Egypt for thousands of years. It was first introduced to England in the 16th Century.

Mint

Reference to find:

*"Woe unto you, scribes and Pharisees, hypocrites! for ye pay tithe of **mint** and anise and cummin,
and have omitted the weightier matters of the law, judgement, mercy and faith:"* Matthew 23:23

Natural History Notes on Mint

Just two mentions in the Bible but widely used by Jews, Greeks and Romans as a flavouring for many dishes. Various species were used with our **Garden Mint (Mentha longifolia), Peppermint and Pennyroyal** popular in those days.

In southern Europe the use of mint in cooking dates back to the Stone Age and just 2000 or so years ago at the time of the birth of Christ the Romans were cultivating a plant believed to have been **Water Mint**.

Water Mint (Mentha aquatica) is common in Britain and Europe and grows in any damp, watery places. Many hybrids including Peppermint have Water Mint as one of their parents. It had numerous medicinal uses particularly against stomach upsets and earache and was an early smelling salt and air freshener. It was sacred to Aphrodite.

Old Country names are Bishopweed, Horse Mint and Lilac Flower.

Horse Mint
(Mentha longifolia)

Mulberry

References to find:

*"Therefore David enquired again of God ; and God said unto him, Go not up after them; turn away from them, and come upon them over against the **mulberry trees**. And it shall be, when thou shalt hear a sound of going in the tops of the **mulberry trees**, that then thou shalt go out to battle:"* 1 Chronicles 14:14,15

*"And the Lord said, If ye had faith as a grain of mustard seed, ye might say unto this **sycamine tree**, Be thou plucked up by the root, and be thou planted in the sea; and it should obey you."* Luke 17:6

Natural History Notes on The Mulberry Tree

The **Black Mulberry (Morus nigra)** is found all over Bible Lands and is the 'sycamine' of Luke, and grown for its large black fruit.

It seems the writers of the Authorised or King James the 1st Version of the Bible called aspens, or poplars, 'mulberries' and called mulberries, 'sycamines' for some obscure reason.

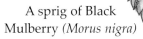

A sprig of Black
Mulberry *(Morus nigra)*

Mustard

References to find:

*"Another parable put he forth unto them, saying, The Kingdom of heaven is like to a grain of **mustard seed**, which a man took and sowed in his field:"* Matthew 13:31

Natural History Notes on Mustard

Black Mustard (Brassica nigra) is of the Crucifereae, the cabbage family and in the Bible Lands grows in great profusion. Mustard groves are such that the plant becomes tall and tree like to the extent birds can and do nest in them, just as is stated in Matthew, 13! The seeds were used to produce oil as well as mustard.

Fields of Black Mustard at sunset on a summer's evening are a magnificent sight even if they do look somewhat alien in the British landscape, though most of the great splashes of yellow field-scapes we see are of rape which produces a more popular mustard.

Black Mustard
(Brassica nigra)

Mustard poultices relieve muscular pains. As youngsters we would soak our feet in mustard baths to help get rid of colds.

Myrrh

Reference to find:

*"Now when every maid's turn was come to go in to king Ahasuerus, after that she had been twelve months, according to the manner of the women, (for so were the days of their purifications accomplished, to wit, six months with oil of **myrrh**, and six months with sweet odours, and with other things for the purifying of the women;) then thus came every maiden unto the king;"* Esther 2:12

Natural History Notes on Myrrh

Everyone knows of Myrrh as one of the gifts to the baby Jesus brought by the wise men but it was first mentioned in the Bible in Exodus. It was also used with powdered Aloe leaves during the embalming of Christ by Nicodemus after Crucifixion, in the garden tomb.

Myrrh is **(Commiphora myrrha)** a fragrant gum which exudes from trees in Abyssinia, Arabia and Somaliland. It is a low, thorny shrub growing in rocky places. It issues from the tree as a rather oily resin which hardens as it reaches the ground.

There is a school of thought that early references to Myrrh links it with ladanum from **Rock Roses (Cistus laurifolius).**

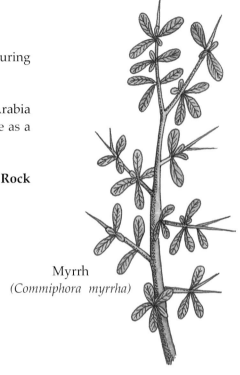

Myrrh
(*Commiphora myrrha*)

Myrtle

Reference to find:

*"…I saw by night, and behold a man riding upon a red horse, and he stood among the **myrtle trees** that were in the bottom; and behind him were there red horses, speckled, and white."* Zechariah 1:8

Natural History Notes on Myrtle

The **Myrtle (Myrtus communis)** is common in Bible Lands and was esteemed for its snowy white flowers, dark green foliage and lovely scent. Its buds and berries used as spices and distilled water prepared from the flowers made it a much loved plant.

It is a small tree or bush with evergreen leaves which are aromatic, the white flowers followed by small, round black berries. It grows wild in southern Europe.

Medicinal uses include the leaves and berries against diarrhoea and dysentery. Also used for spitting of the blood, catarrh, and dropped womb problems.

A sprig of Myrtle
(*Myrtus communis*)

Nettles

References to find:

"Among the bushes they brayed;
*Under the **nettles** they were gathered together."* Job 30:7

"For, lo, they are gone because of destruction : Egypt shall gather them up, Memphis shall bury them:
*the pleasant places for their silver, **nettles** shall possess them: thorns shall be in their tabernacles."* Hosea 9:6

Natural History Notes on Nettles

Acanthus
(Acanthus spinosus)

So was the plant a nettle as we know them or was it indeed **Acanthus spinosus**, a rapidly growing bush according to King Solomon, large enough to shelter the so-called outcasts. Today the **acanthus** grows densely with tall spikes of beautiful flowers and leaves so delightfully formed as to have inspired Greek architecture and church carvings here in Britain too. Coins were fashioned in silver depicting this plant.

Stinging nettles do grow in Bible Lands and our own **Common Nettle, (Urtica dioica)** is a widespread species which has been both loved and reviled since prehistoric days. Used for a cloth like linen, and for food and a medicine, the nettle is a fabulous plant and very beautiful.

The dried leaves make nettle tea and fresh young leaves are steamed and eaten like spinach. Nettle stings cure rheumatism and during the Second World War nettles were harvested to supply chlorophyll for medicines.

I have seen nettles growing to 6ft (180cms) tall but cannot imagine anyone sheltering beneath them. Old country names include; Devil's Plaything, Hoky Poky, Hidgy Pidgy and Jenny Nettle.

So, we must stay with Acanthus spinosus which was named from the Greek 'akanthos' for prickle though here it grows only to about 4ft (120cms). It was introduced from Southern Europe in 1548 and is sometimes known as Bear's Breeches and Elephant's Ears. Its leaves are evergreen.

And in comparison…
Common Nettle
(Urtica dioica)

Oak

References to find:

*"And Joshua wrote these words in the book of the law of God, and took a great stone, and set it up there under an **oak**, that was by the sanctuary of the Lord"* Joshua 24:26

Natural History Notes on the Oak Tree

The **Holm Oak (Quercus ilex)** or **Holly Oak**, which grows as planted specimens in many parts of Britain is a delightful evergreen I know well, with its whispering leaves.

With six oaks in Palestine and those in the Bible are usually 'oak' with little further identification except perhaps location. Abraham dwelt in the plain by the oaks. The Palestinian ilex is a native of the Mediterranean region and may reach a height of 50ft (16m) in Palestine and Syria. The acorns are edible, the timber used for farm implements and cart wheels. One could speculate on Christ, as a carpenter following Joseph, his father's trade, working Holm Oak wood. The tree is a bit of a loner usually but there are forests of it in Corsica evidently.

And in comparison…
'Our' English Oak
(Quercus robur)

The Holm Oak
(Quercus ilex)

The **Valonia Oak (Quercus Ægilops)** is an oak getting its name from the Greek for acorn. The acorns are huge, reaching 2.5ins (7.0cms) long and 3ins (7.5cms) in girth! The acorn cups provide a black dye. It is widely spread throughout Asia Minor, Crete, Syria and Palestine.

Abraham's Oak (Q. coccifera. var. palestina). A sample at Kew had an estimated age of 700 years and is said to have been a great branch of Abraham's Oak which fell in deep snow in the winter of 1856-57. It was presented to Kew by Mrs. Finn, wife of the British consul at Jerusalem at that time. The tree would have sent it's first shoot from its acorn at the time of the second Crusade around 150 AD.

Olive

"Although the fig tree shall not blossom,
Neither shall fruit be in the vines;
*The labour of the **olive** shall fail,*
And the fields shall yield no meat;"
Habakkuk 3:17

*"… Go forth unto the mount, and fetch **olive** branches,*
and pine branches, and myrtle branches, and palm branches,
and branches of thick trees, to make booths as it is written."
Nehemiah 8:15

Natural History Notes on the Olive Tree

An essential tree of Bible Lands and a common and very beautiful tree it is, very closely linked with human lives. A single Olive tree can supply a whole family with the fats it needs. The Olive branch is a symbol of peace and the oil anointed the heads of kings, yet it was an everyman's tree and it lives to a great age.

Actually there are several varieties of Olive in Bible Lands and all have leathery green leaves and small, white flowers. Olive groves and Olive gardens are so much a part of Palestine.

The Olive Tree
(Olea europaea)

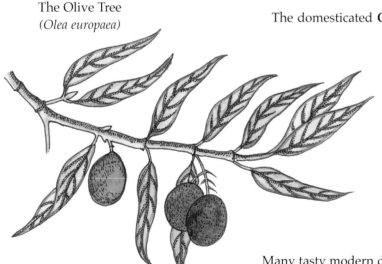

The domesticated **Olive tree (Olea europaea)** has thrived in the Mediterranean region since prehistoric times and thus produces one of the oldest fruits known. It is an evergreen, flowering in springtime and producing autumn berries. It does not need rich soil, flourishing on stony ground wherever a Mediterranean type climate exists.

The difference between green and black olives is ripeness. Unripe olives are green, fully ripe olives are black. They need to be cured to remove the bitterness and each has its own curing method. Green olives must be soaked in a lye solution before brining while black olives can be brined straight away.

Many tasty modern dishes including pizzas are made using olives.

Pistachio Nut Tree

References to find:

"And their father Israel said unto them, If it must be so now, do this; take of the best fruits in the land in your vessels, and carry down the man a present, a little balm, and a little honey, spices, and myrrh, **nuts** *and almonds:"* Genesis 43:11

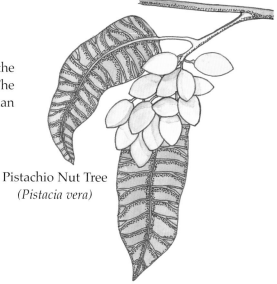

Natural History Notes on the Pistachio Nut Tree

Supplies of this nut still come from Bible Lands. The wild tree has many relations including the **Turpentine tree, Pistacia terebinthus** and various **Rhus** species as well as the true **Sumac**. The **mastich tree** providing resin that is chewed by locals is **Pistacia lentisens** and more bush than tree like. Tooth picks are made from the wood which must help the chewers.

Pistachio Nut Tree
(Pistacia vera)

Shittah – Acacia Tree

Reference to find:

"I will plant in the wilderness the cedar, the **shittah tree**, *and the myrtle, and the oil tree;"* Isaiah 41:19

Natural History Notes on the Shittah Tree

Said to be the tree used for the Ark as well as the fittings for the Tabernacle this tree is an important soil improver as its roots impregnate the soil with nitrogen. Thus in its way it is a 'nursery' tree helping other species to grow.

Speculation as to the probability this could be the 'burning bush' associated with Moses brings about two interesting theories. One is that summer lightning sometimes plays lightly over rock outcrops and trees for several seconds, lighting the trunks and foliage but doing no real harm.

Some Botanicals, however, believe that the extraordinary phenomenon of the first flush of spring can be so rapid in desert situations as to produce a sudden bursting of fiery red leaves during which they are unable to form chlorophyll fast enough to keep up with the speed of their 'bursting' out. A remarkable sight that must be.

(The Shittah Tree)
The Acacia Tree
(Acacia seyal)

Palm Tree

Reference to find:

*"The righteous shall flourish like the **palm tree**:*
He shall grow like a cedar in Lebanon." Psalm 92:12

"The vine is dried up, and the fig tree languisheth; the pomegranate tree,
*the **palm tree** also, and the apple tree, even all the trees of the field, are withered."* Joel 1:12

Natural History Notes on the Palm Tree

Palms, still plentiful in Egypt are now scarce in Palestine yet they were once so abundant. Jericho was the 'City of Palms' and the Jordan Valley was covered with date palms.

The **Palm Tree, Pheonix dactylifera**, had both important practical uses and symbolic significance. So graceful was it that girls were named Tamar after its Hebrew name. It may reach 100ft (30m) in height and is crowned not with branches but with fan-shaped leaves beneath which grow the dates in clusters.

The palm provides sugar, oil, wax, starch and fruit. Its leaves make mats when woven and its fibres make paper, and threads for sewing. In the desert it indicates the presence of water - a wonderful tree.

In some British counties Palm is a name given to the Yew Tree.

Date Palm Tree
(Pheonix dactylifera)

130

Plane Tree

References to find:

*"The cedars in the garden of God could not hide him: the fir trees were not like his boughs, and the **chestnut** trees were not like his branches; nor any tree in the garden of God was like unto him in his beauty."* Ezekiel 31:8

Oriental Plane Tree
(Platanus orientalis)

Natural History Notes on the Plane Tree

In the Authorised Version of the Bible there is a reference in Genesis to the **Chestnut tree**, though the Septuagint and the English Revised Version says **Plane**. This tree is abundant in Palestine and has been regarded as a great purifier of air, even to preventing plague and other diseases. The fruit, leaves and bark have all been highly regarded medicinally. (See Chestnut.)

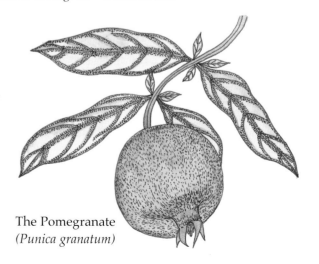

Pomegranate

Reference to find:

*"And Saul tarried in the uttermost part of Gibeah under a **pomegranate tree** which is in Migron:"* 1 Samuel 14:2

Natural History Notes on the Pomegranate

Mentioned many times in the Bible, useful and popular and not a native to Palestine though now common there. It probably derives from Afghanistan via Syria and Iran and grown in Egypt for thousands of years.

The **Pomegranate (Punica granatum)** tree is but a small bush-like tree with deep green leaves and scarlet flowers. The pulp of the fruit is used for making drinks yet the rind cures tapeworms and is used for leather tanning. Books that are Morocco bound are from leather tanned with pomegranate rind processes.

The Pomegranate
(Punica granatum)

Poplar

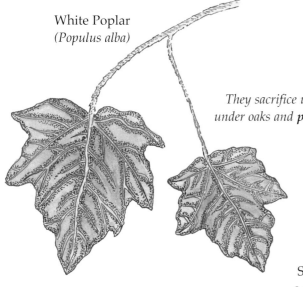

White Poplar
(Populus alba)

References to find:

*They sacrifice upon the tops of the mountains, and burn incense upon the hills,
under oaks and **poplars** and elms, because the shadow thereof is good:"* Hosea 4:13

Natural History Notes on the Poplar

The **White Poplar (Populus alba)** is one of several species growing in the Bible Lands, reaching a height of 30-60ft (10-20m). The catkin flowers appear before the leaves and the buds are covered with a resinous varnish.

Stand beneath a White Poplar on a breezy day in Britain to hear the leaves tremble with a sound like pattering rain. A tree that flourishes near the sea it is now widely planted as an 'ornamental'. It is native to the Old World from Western Europe to Central Asia and may have been brought here from Holland in the 16th century. Male flowers are crimson, female flowers green and both appear before the leaves on separate trees.

The eggs of the Goat Moth are laid in the bark of white poplars. (See also 'Willow')

Rie (Spelt)

Reference to find:

*"When he hath made plain the face thereof, doth he not cast abroad the fitches, and scatter the cummin,
and cast in the principal wheat and the appointed barley and the **rie** in their place?"* Isaiah 28:25

(Rie) Rye
(Secale cereale)

Natural History Notes on Rie (Spelt)

Biblical Rie was probably Spelt which grows in soil too poor even for grass to survive. Bread made from Spelt may be inferior to that of wheat but it will grow in soil not rich enough for wheat so it is indeed a useful grain crop.

Rose

Reference to find:

*"The wilderness and the solitary place shall be glad for them; and the desert shall rejoice, and blossom as the **rose**."* Isaiah 35:1

Natural History Notes on the Rose

The so-called Rose of the Bible is not a rose of the genus Rosa that we know. Today the view is that the **narcissus (Narcissus tazetta)** is the plant, i.e the white or polyanthus narcissus, an abundant species of Bible Lands. It actually has brilliant golden flowers in hot areas and these are white in cooler climates.

and… The Phoenician Rose
(Rosa phoenicia)

Biblical Roses
(Narcissus tazetta)

Rose of Sharon

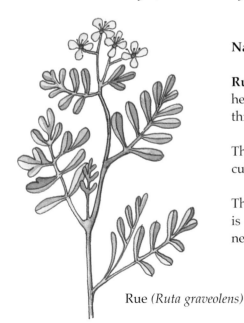

Reference to find:

*"I am the **rose of Sharon,***
And the lily of the valleys." Song of Solomon 2:1

Natural History Notes on the Rose of Sharon

Another mis-interpretation it seems! The Rose of Sharon of the Song of Solomon is identified as the **Mountain tulip (Tulipa montana)** or sharon tulip **(Tulipa sharonensis)** which grows in the hills and plains between Carmel and Jaffa. The plant has silvery green leaves and red, glowingly beautiful flowers richer on the inside than without.

The Rose of Sharon
Mountain Tulip
(Tulipa sharonensis)

Rue

Reference to find:

*"But woe unto you, Pharisees! For ye tithe mint and **Rue** and all manner of herbs, and pass over judgement and the love of God:"* Luke 11:42

Natural History Notes on Rue

Ruta graveolens, the **Rue** was greatly prized by the ancients for its smell drove away plagues, healed bee stings and the bites of serpents it is said. It is strong smelling, has grey-green leaves throughout the year and yellow flowers in summer.

The tithe reference in Luke tells of its cultivation, for wild plants were free of tithe until they were cultivated.

The seed taken in wine is an antidote against all dangerous medicines and poisons, it is said. It is combined with nerve tonics such as skullcap and valerian, today, as a remedy for many nervous conditions including headaches, dizziness and palpitations.

Rue *(Ruta graveolens)*

Rush

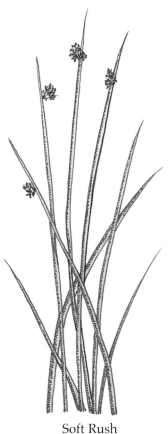

Reference to find:

*"Can the **rush** grow up without mire?*
Can the flag grow without water? Job 8:11.

Natural History Notes on the Rush

The Rush of Job is thought to be the **Soft Rush (Juncus effusus)** which is found in most wet places in Bible Lands. It grows to about 5ft (150cm) and is common, too, in Britain and Europe, especially on acid soils. In Bible Lands it has been used for centuries to make baskets.

It had its uses here, strewn on stone floors of houses to provide some warmth before the days of carpets. The pith used to be taken from the stems and made into wicks for candles.

Medicinally Soft Rush seeds were immersed in water, then mixed with wine as a cold cure.

The plant grows with upright shoots and finely ridged stems, in tufts. It flowers from June to August, the flowers being an attractive olive green in colour.

Soft Rush
(Juncus effusus)

Saffron

Reference to find:

"Thy plants are an orchard of pomegranates, with pleasant fruits;
*Camphire, with spikenard, Spikenard and **saffron**;*
Calamus and cinnamon, with all trees of frankincense;" Song of Solomon 4:13,14

Natural History Notes on Saffron

Just one mention of **Saffron (Crocus sativus)** in the Bible and that in the Song of Solomon.

Saffron is from the Arabic zafran meaning yellow and is the deep orange-yellow substance contained in the stigmas. 4,000 stigmas are required to make 1 oz of saffron. It was long used in curries and stews and to make a yellow dye. Cake saffron is made by drying tightly packed stigmas in the sun.

Saffron
(*Crocus sativus*)

Sycamore

Reference to find:

*"And he ran before, and climbed up into a **sycomore tree** to see him: for he was to pass that way."* Luke 19:4

Natural History Notes on the Sycamore Tree

Legend tells us that the sycamore was brought from the East during the time of the Crusades. It was thought to be the tree climbed by Zacchaeus in the Gospels though we know it was not the species we know as the sycamore. It is likely the tree was a species known as **Ficus sycamorus**, a species of **Fig**, or the **Black Mulberry,** though the fig is generally accepted.

Interestingly this particular fig is not common in Bible Lands whilst the Black Mulberry is abundant and still known as sycominus in Greece. It is still thought by some to be the tree referred to by St.Luke. (See Fig)

It does seem unlikely 'our' **sycamore (Acer pseudoplatanus)** reached Britain during the Crusades as it seeds so freely one would have thought it would have been more common by the end of the 16th century. When Gerard wrote in his Herball it was a stranger to England. He referred to it as the 'Great Maple' and the 'sycamore'.

'Our' Sycamore
(*Acer pseudoplatanus*)

Spikenard

References to find:

*"Then took Mary a pound of ointment of **spikenard**, very costly, and anointed the feet of Jesus, and wiped his feet with her hair: and the house was filled with the odour of the ointment."* John 12:3

Natural History Notes on Spikenard

The Biblical Spikenard comes from the stem of the **Himalayan Valerian** which grows in the mountains of Nepal. It is a very precious perfume kept in alabastar containers to preserve the scent. The plant here is **Nardostachys jatamansi**.

Our own **Common Valerian (Valeriana officinalis)** was also used similarly in the Middle Ages, the dried roots used as a spice and a perfume. The roots were also placed in drawers to keep linen smelling fresh and clean.

During World War 1 the juice of fresh Valerian roots was used to calm people following air raids.

'Our' Common Valerian
(Valeriana officinalis)

Tares

Reference to find:

*Another parable put he forth unto them, saying, The kingdom of heaven is likened unto a man which sowed good seed in his field: but while men slept his enemy came and sowed **tares** among the wheat, and went his way."* Matthew 13:24,25

Darnel Grass
(Lolium temulentum)

Natural History Notes on Tares

A weed which grew in wheat fields, the darnel grass, a problem in the Near East but sometimes, too, in the wheat fields of England today. It is a kind of **rye grass (Lolium temulentum)** with Lolium meaning 'darnel' in Latin.

Not to be confused with **Hairy Tare, Vicia hirsuta,** a tiny vetch-like member of the Pea family common in grassy places in Britain, and on cultivated ground.

Thorns & Thistles

Reference to find:

"And unto Adam he said, Because thou hast hearkened unto the voice of thy wife, and hast eaten of the tree, of which I commanded thee, saying, Thou shalt not eat of it: cursed is the ground for thy sake; in sorrow shalt thou eat of it all the days of thy life; thorns also and **thistles** *shall it bring forth to thee;"* Genesis 3:17,18

Natural History Notes on Thorns & Thistles

Frequently mentioned in the Bible but impossible to identify. There are a lot of Thorns and Thistles out there!

An Example of Thistles.

Wheat

References to find:

*"And that which they have need of, both young bullocks, and rams, and lambs, for the burnt offerings of the God of heaven, **wheat**, salt, wine, and oil, according to the appointment of the priests which are at Jerusalem, let it be given them day by day without fail:* Ezra 6:9

Example of wheat.
Durum Wheat
(Triticum durum)

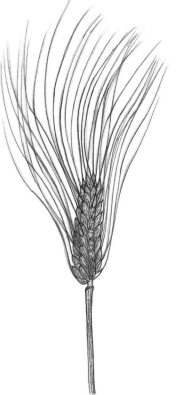

Natural History Notes on Wheat

Vitally important and reference to cereal crops are many. The quality of wheat in the Bible Lands was and is good and cultivation methods still include flail threshing, oxen treading and winnowing with sifters and a fan. Sickles are still used for harvesting around June time, the biggest dread being drought.

Willow

Reference to find:

*"For I will pour water upon him that is thirsty, and floods upon the dry ground: I will pour my spirit upon thy seed, and my blessing upon thine offspring: and they shall spring up as among the grass, as **willow** by the water courses."*
Isaiah 44:3,4

Natural History Notes on Willow

The **Willow** of the Israelites exiles is **Populus euphratica** and is a variable species and a true native of Bible Lands, and capable of attaining 50ft (17m) in height. Its leaves have a grey-green colour on both sides and on young trees are linear or oblong short stalked and typically willow-like. Leaves on old trees vary greatly and are often long stalked, ovate, oblong, or quite round.

However, it is thought that the Jews in captivity hung their harps on poplars that grow by the rivers of Babylon and well know on banks of shallow rivers from Syria to Palestine and especially common in the Jordan valley. They may attain a height of 40ft (13m) and have small heart-shaped leaves and tiny green catkins in early spring.

(See also 'Poplar')

and in comparison…
'Our' White Willow (*Salix alba*)

The Euphrates Poplar, also called Aspen Willow
(*Populus euphratica*)

Wormwood

References to find:

*"Behold, I will feed them, even this people, with **wormwood**, and give them water of gall to drink."* Jeremiah 9:15

*"He hath filled me with bitterness, he hath made me drunken with **wormwood**."* Lamentations 3:15

Natural History Notes on Wormwood

Frequently referred to in the Bible and known for its bitterness. A bitter juice is produced from **Artemisia judaica**, named from the Greek goddess Artemis and well known for many centuries. One variety was known as the **virgin plant**, or **parthenia**. The various species in the genus tend to look alike. In ancient times the herb was steeped in wine to counteract the effect of alcohol.

Our English **Wormwood** we know as **Mugwort**, a fairly common wayside plant growing to the size of a small shrub. The leaves taste bitter and are used medicinally. **Artemisia vulgaris** it is

called and the plant has a pleasant aromatic odour. It makes a strong tea and is a good moth repellent when laid in clothes.

"If they'd drink nettles in March
And Mugwort in May
So many fine maidens
Would not turn to clay."

'Our' Wormwood, Mugwort
(*Artemisia vulgaris*)

Yellow Flag Iris

Reference to find:

"And the daughter of Pharaoh came down to wash herself at the river;
and her maidens walked along by the river's side;
*and when she saw the ark among the **flags**, she sent her maid to fetch it."*

Exodus 2:5

Natural History Notes on Yellow Flag Iris

Evening sunlight on the marshes in summer, yellow flag iris in abundance along the water's edge as sedge and reed warblers sing and a kingfisher perches, swaying, on a willow branch…. England 2007 AD.

As Job said, "Can the flag grow without water?" and it is true, **Iris pseudacorus** is part and parcel of our wetlands in shallow waters on the edges of dykes, ditches and streams, even in wet woodlands, just as are irises everywhere.

The Yellow flag we know so well is not a Palestinian plant but the **Nazareth Iris, (Iris nazarena)** and **Costet's Iris (Iris costeti)** make springtime in Galilee very beautiful.

The yellow iris has parts in threes reminding us of the Trinity. The petals and sepals are all yellow and petal-like. The three styles are also petal like, forming the uppermost, crested 'petals'. It is now the flower of the fleur-de-lys, the Iris adopted by Louis VII in his crusade against the Saracens.

Iris is Greek for 'Rainbow'. Yellow flag leaves are sharp and can cut the careless, hence an old name, Sword Flag. The plant is mainly pollinated by bees. After pollination the petals fall away to reveal a large green seed capsule. This stalk begins to bend and the capsule eventually splits to reveal a mass of yellow-brown seeds.

Old country names include daggers (from the leaves) Duck's Bill, Jacob's Sword, Trinity, Queen of the Marshes, Water Segg, Lavers (Old English, Laefer) and Dragon Flower.

It is a special herb of St.John's Eve and averts evil. The rhizomes give a black dye and black ink whilst the roasted seeds produce a healthy drink not unlike coffee. It was also used as an astringent to stop the flow of blood.

'Our' Yellow Flag Iris
(*Iris pseudacorus*)

Index

FAUNA

Accipiter badius 27
Accipiter gentilis 27
Accipiter nisus 27
Addax nasomaculatus 79
Alectoris chukar 21
Allolobophora longa 91
Allolobophora nocturna 91
Ammoperdix leyi 21
Apis Mellifera 86
Apodemus sylvaticus 76
Apus apus 24
Aquila chrysaetos 33
Aquila heliaca 33
Araneus diadematus 88
Ardea cinerea 25, 26
Ardea purpurea 25
Athene noctua 31, 32
Atta barbara 78
Atta structor 78
Botaurus stellaris 26
Buteo buteo 29
Canis aureus 64, 65
Canis familiaris leineri 68, 69
Canis lupus lupus 63, 64

Capra aegagrus 61
Capra hircus aegagrus 61
Capra nubiana 61
Capreolus capreolus 59, 60
Caprimulgus europaeus 19
Cervus elaphus 60
Chamaeleo chameleon 62
Ciconia ciconia 38
Ciconia nigra 38
Circaetus gallicus 33
Clamator glandarius 17
Columba palumbus 15
Columbicola columbae 89
Corpis lunaris 87
Corvus corax 12, 13
Corvus ruficollis 13
Coturnix coturnix 20
Cuculus canorus 17
Culex pipiens 83, 84
Cygnus bewickii 40
Cygnus cygnus 40
Cygnus olor 40
Dama dama 60
Eptesicus serotinus 74
Equus africanus 54

Equus asinus 54
Equus caballus 53
Erinaceus europaeus 63
Falco tinnunculus 28
Fennecus zerda) 67
Grus grus 39
Gypeatus barbatus 35
Gyps fulvus 35
Haemopis sanquisuba 91
Helix aspersa 90
Helix pomatia 90
Hieraaetus fasciatus 33, 34
Hirudo medicinalis 91
Hirundo rustica 24
Hyaena hyaena 65
Iridomyrmex humilis 78
Lacerta vivipara 48
Lasius niger 78, 79
Lepus capensis europaeus 77
Lepus europeus syriacus 77
Locusta migratoria 81, 82
Mandragorga Officinarum 6
Meles meles 72
Mellivora capensis 72
Menopon gallinae 89

Milvus migrans 30
Milvus milvus 29, 30
Monomorium pharaonis 78
Mustela nivalis 74
Naja haje 47
Neophron percnopterus 35
Nycticorax nycticorax 25
Oryctolagus cuniculus 66
Ovis ammon ophion 62
Ovis aries 57
Ovis musimon 57
Pandion haliaetus 28
Panthera leo 71
Panthera pardus 70
Papio hamadryas 45
Passer domesticus 18
Passer montanus 18
Pavo cristatus 36
Pediculus humanus 88, 89
Pediculus humanus capitis 88
Pelecanus onocrotalus 37
Perdix perdix 21
Phalacrocorax carbo 15, 16
Pipistrellus pipistrellus 74

Plegadis falcinellus 40
Procavia capensis syriacus 66
Ptyodactylus gecko 49
Pulex irritans 85
Rana esculenta 51
Rana punctata 51
Rana temporaria 51
Rupicapra rupicapra 62
Spalax ehrenbergi 75
Spalax microphthalmus
    ehrenbergi 75
Streptopelia decaocto 14, 15
Streptopelia turtur 14
Struthio camelus 37
Sus scrofa 56
Tachyorctes splendens 75
Talpa europaea 75
Testudo greaca 50
Theobaldia annulata 85
Tineola bisselliella 84
Torgos tracheliotus 35
Trocheta subviridis 91
Trogium pulsatorium 89
Truxalis grandis 83
Tyto alba 11, 31, 32
Upupa epops 23
Ursus arctos 73
Vanellus vanellus 23
Varanus griseus 48
Vespa crabro 87
Vespa orientalis 86
Vipera aspis 48
Vipera berus 46
Vipera lebetina lebetina 46
Vipera xanthina 46
Vulpes vulpes 67
Vulpes vulpes niloticus 67

FLORA
Acacia seyal 130
Acanthus spinosus 126
Acer pseudoplatanus 136
Aesculus hippocastanum 107
Agrostemma githago 108
Allium sativum 113
Aloe barbadense 94
Anemone coronaria 120
Aquilaria agallocha 94
Artemisia judaica 140
Artemisia vulgaris 140, 141
Atriplex halimus 121
Balanites aegyptiaca 97
Brassica nigra 124
Bryonia dioica 121
Buxus longifolia 100
Cedrus libani 105
Cinnamomum cassia 104
Cinnamomum verum 107
Cinnamomum zeylanicum
    107
Cistus laurifolius 125
Citrullus vulgaris 122
Commiphora gileadensis 97
Commiphora myrrha 125
Commiphora opobalsamum
    97
Conium maculatum 116
Convallaria majalis 119
Coriandrum sativum 109
Corylus avellana 115
Crocus sativus 135, 136
Cucumis sativus 110
Diospyros ebenaster 111
Diospyros ebenum 111
Dolichos lablab 99

Ficus carica 111, 112
Ficus sycamorus 136
Hordeum vulgare 98
Hyssopus officinalis 116, 117
Iris costeti 142
Iris nazarena 142
Iris pseudacorus 141, 142
Juncus effusus 135
Juniperus chinensis 118
Juniperus communis 118
Laurus nobilis 98, 99
Lawsonia inermis 104
Lens culinaris 119
Lens esculenta 119
Lignum rhodianum, 96
Lilium candidum 120
Linum bienne 113
Linum catharticum 112, 113
Linum perenne 113
Linum usitatissimum 112
Lolium temulentum 137
Malus sylvestris 96
Melissa officinalis 97
Mentha aquatica 123
Mentha longifolia 123
Morus nigra 123
Myrtus communis 125
Narcissus tazetta 133
Nardostachys jatamansi 137
Olea europaea 128
Origanum maru 117
Origanum vulgare 117
Pheonix dactylifera 130
Pistacia lentisens 129
Pistacia vera 129
Platanus orientalis 106, 131
Platanus X hispanica 106

Podophyllum peltatum 121
Populus alba 132
Populus euphratica 97, 139,
    140
Prunus amygdalus 95
Prunus armenaica 96
Prunus dulcis 95
Prunus laurocerasus 107
Punica granatum 131
Pyrus communis 96
Quercus Ægilops 127
Quercus coccifera 127
Quercus ilex 127
Quercus robur 127
Retama raetum 117
Rosa phoenicia 133
Rubus fruticosus 101
Rubus ulmifolius 101
Ruta graveolens 134
Salix alba 140
Saussurea lappa 104
Secale cereale 132
Solanum dulcamara 102
Solanum incanum 102
Solanum nigrum 102
Triticum durum 6, 139
Tulipa montana 134
Tulipa sharonensis 134
Typha augustifolia 103
Typha latifolia 103
Urtica dioica 126
Valeriana officinalis 137
Vicia faba 99
Vicia hirsuta 138
Vitis vinifera 114